POWERFUL

INSPIRATIONS

POWERFUL INSPIRATIONS

EIGHT LESSONS THAT

WILL CHANGE YOUR LIFE

by KATHY IRELAND

and LAURA MORTON

GALILEE

DOUBLEDAY

NEW YORK   LONDON   TORONTO   SYDNEY   AUCKLAND

A GALILEE BOOK
PUBLISHED BY DOUBLEDAY
a division of Random House, Inc.
1745 Broadway, New York, New York 10019

GALILEE, DOUBLEDAY, and the portrayal of a ship with a
cross above a book are trademarks of Random House, Inc.

First Galilee edition published February 2004

Book design by Margaret M. Wagner

The Library of Congress has cataloged the Doubleday hardcover
edition as follows:
Ireland, Kathy.
Powerful Inspirations : eight lessons that will change your life
/ by Kathy Ireland and Laura Morton.—1st ed.
p. cm

1. Christian Women—Religious life. I. Morton, Laura.
II. Title.
BV4527 1642002
158—dc21   2001058404

ISBN 0-385-50308-3

This book is dedicated
to the love of my life,
my amazing husband,
Greg,
and the lights of our lives,
our incredible children,
Erik, Lily, and Chloe.

CONTENTS

◈   ◈

ACKNOWLEDGMENTS
ix

FOREWORD
Laura Morton
xvii

INTRODUCTION
Kathy Ireland
xxiii

Chapter One
POWERFUL INSPIRATIONS
I

Chapter Two
POWERFUL YOU
15

Contents

◈ ◈

Chapter Three

POWERFUL FAMILIES

43

Chapter Four

POWERFUL ANSWERS

69

Chapter Five

POWERFUL CHANGES

95

Chapter Six

POWERFUL FINANCIAL WISDOM

115

Chapter Seven

POWERFUL BELIEFS AND
BOUNDARIES

139

Chapter Eight

POWERFUL JOYS AND SORROWS

153

Powerful Inspirations

LESSON RECAP

177

ACKNOWLEDGMENTS

❖   ❖

Trust in the Lord with all your heart
and lean not on your own understanding;
in all your ways acknowledge him,
and He will make your paths straight.

PROVERBS 3:5–6

In order to accomplish things we need the love and
support of others. I would like to thank the following,
without whose help this book would not be possible.

My Lord, Savior, and best friend, Jesus Christ.

My Granny, Granddad, Grandpa Gus, and Uncle
Richard are special members of our family who I will
always love, remember, and appreciate. I want to keep
their memory alive for generations to come with
stories of their love and adventures. I am saddened

they did not live to know my wonderful new family members.

Here's a look at our family tree: My beautiful Grandma Gladys finds a silver lining in every cloud—she always communicates love. My wonderful Auntie Dorothy, Dad's sister, has always been a pillar of strength for us. As children, we spent so much time with her, and she continues to inspire us all with her love of life and love of others. The entire Niemann family, Mom's beloved sisters and brothers, Uncle Fritz, Aunt Linda, Aunt Camilla, Uncle Bill, Uncle Greg, Aunt Leila, Uncle Joe, Aunt Laurie, Uncle Tom, Aunt Jeri, Uncle Matt, Aunt Betty, Aunt Mary, Uncle Ron, Uncle Jim, and Aunt Sue, you are each so special to me. My mom and dad, my husband, Greg, our children, Erik and Lily, my sister, Mary, her husband, Sal, and Anthony, Paul, and Julia, my sister, Cynthia, her husband, Mark, Phil and Barbara, the best in-laws I could ever wish for, Greg's brother, Grant, his wife, Dyan, and our nephew, Wyatt, Greg's sister, Dana, her husband, Paul, and our nephews, Jacob, Joseph, and baby Jr., thank you for your love and for always being there for me. All of my incredible cousins and their children, our relatives from England, Norway, Canada, Utah, and Texas, I love you all.

❖ ❖

My friends Joe Antonini, the Bacas and their extended families, Jerry and Dotty Bartrand, Ed, Rachelle, Nick, Amanda, and Hayden Begley, Lee Benedict, Baret and Judi Boisson, Kim Branch, Art and Bonnie Burke, Jule and Ron Campbell, Charles Chini, Miles Cooley, Joy Corneliussen, MaryJane Cumino and Kevin, Lisa, Dave, Justin, Jessica, Joelle, and Jacob DeLong, Dale, Julia, Nick and Meehan Dellar, John DiGiuseppe, Vanessa Ergas, Felipa Espinosa, Sim, Debbie, Justin, and Joel Farar, Warren Flick, Dawn Gallagher, Andy, Wanda, Vanessa, and Andy Jr. Giancamilli, Floyd and Jan Hall, Donna Haskell, Sam, Mary, Sam IV, and MaryLane Haskell, Florence Jokstad, Cecil Kearse, Don Keeble, Vanessa and Andrew Kishino, Scott Klusendorf, Bill, Donna, Billy, Scott, and Mark Kuchmas, Frankie Mayer, Betty Mazetti and Stan Hatch, Rick and Wendy Mokler, Jeannine Morgan, everyone from school, Michelene Mundo, Rachel Naples, the Orr Family, Bill, Jennifer, Brianna, and Taylor Paulson, Dave, Sue, Whitney, Parker, and Lakey Peterson, Maria Rodriguez, Steve Rosenblum and Adrian Ponce, Steven Ross, Cindy and Joe Sapienza, Jaclyn Smith, Captain Adrian, Dayle, Ann, Charles, Minky, and Catherine Tarte and Bertie, Jeannie Teplansky, Mike Teplansky, Joan van Ark and Jack Marshall, Adelaide Veverka and Camille, Peter, Isabella, Fred,

❖ ❖

and Sam Ysebrands. Thank you for your love and friendship.

Some very special young people: Claire Eva and Noah Mathew Benjamin, Brittany Duncan, Brent Allen Mickelson, Blaise Meeke, Trinity Carthen, Eva Cisneros, Bianca Lauren DiGiuseppe, Marie-Clotilde Ergas, Brittany McDaniels, Laura and Charles Moretz.

My business partners, past and present, including John and Marilyn Moretz and the Moretz Mills Team, with whom it all began; the Hogdson Family and everyone at Kathy Ireland Home by Standard; the Shaw and Saul Families, Warren Buffet, and the incredible team at Shaw Industries; the Pacific Coast Lighting Team; the Next Dimension Studios Team; George Eouse, Ben Torres, and the AFD Décor Team; the Kathy Ireland Home by Lady Americana Team; the Martin Family and the Kathy Ireland Home by the Martin Team; the Kamenstein Team at Lifetime Hoan; Steve, Lynn, and the Kathy Ireland Home by the Alta Team; ACafe, by my friend Chef Andre Carthen; Jardin du Jour, cultivated by Nicholas Walker; Martin Gruber, Fred, and the Kathy Ireland Jewelry by the Gruber Team.

ACKNOWLEDGMENTS

◈ ◈

My partners at KIWW and SWC, Erik and Jason, Jon and Stephen, and Steve. My genius team at KIWW and SWC past and present, Sandy Aguillon, Joel Blitz, Tony Carnot, Melissa Ciampa, Melvin Cisneros, Charlie, Danielle, and Nina Corbo, Claude Ergas, Allison Francis, Rocco Ingemi, Matthew Larsen, Konrad Leh, David Miles, Florentina Morales, Richard Morales, Zulma Ponce, Miles Robinson, Jim Scalfani, Lori Skalabrin, Mitch Sternard, Dee and Georgia, Eva and Viola, you live in our hearts, I love you all.

Tom Law and Company for terrific support and your role in our wonderful partnerships.

Our legal team: John Kenosian and Associates, Donna Melby and the team at Sonneschein Nath and Rosenthal, thank you for your attention to detail and working with my teams every step of the way.

Peter, Brad, Younghee, Michelle, Jean, and everyone at Tanner, Mainstain, Hoffer and Peyrot, Stephen Miny and everyone at New Act Travel, Dick Guttman and Associates, Miriam Wizman, Bill Desser, and Chris Spencer, all that you do is greatly appreciated.

Tim Green for friendship and guiding my fitness career.

Anthony Robbins for generously helping me strengthen my ability to communicate.

For the cover photograph, I'd like to thank my friend, Jonathan Exley for his talent and the talents of each member of the photo team, my friend, Gayle Susan Baizer for wardrobe and styling, my friends, Ken Paves for hair styling and Kara Yoshimoto for make-up, thank you for your friendship and talent.

I must also thank my talented friends, Richard Hume, Charles Bush, Randee St. Nicholas, James Loy, Matthew Van Leeuwen, Oribe, Fran Cooper, Saturo, Katja Cahill, and Rosemary Redlin.

Martin Delaney and everyone at Project Inform, Elise Kim and everyone at Athletes and Entertainers for Kids, the Shriver Family and the Special Olympics, Barbara Ireland Walk for the Cure benefiting the Susan Love MD Foundation with special thanks to Uncle Tom and Aunt Jeri, Elaine Kay and the Santa Barbara Therapeutic Riding Academy, Tom Rollerson and The Dream Foundation Team, The Santa Barbara

Rescue Mission, Life Network, Susan Ham and The Homeless Educational Liaison Project, The Arthritis Foundation, and Feed the Children, your love of others inspires us all.

Pastor Bruce and Marilu Greene, Eunice Kennedy Shriver, Marilyn McCoo and Billy Davis, Jr., Jessica Simpson, Rev. Robert Schuller, Bill Cosby, Shaquille O'Neal, and Martha Williamson, thank you for your kindness.

Mel Berger and everyone at William Morris Agency, thank you for your support and enthusiasm.

The entire team at Doubleday, including our editor, Trace Murphy, his former assistant, Siobhan Dunn, as well as his new assistant, Joan Schadt, Eric Major, Beth Dickey, and Alexandra Beatty Morris, thank you for great team work.

To my friend and co-author, Laura Morton, who stayed strong as we faced challenges in making this book a reality. May this be the first of many collaborations. Thank you for your talent and passion.

Thank you to each person who communicates with me through my website, kathyireland.com and to everyone who has made our brand growth possible, especially busy moms, you are heroes to me.

Even with all the people who are mentioned here, there are many I love who are not. I hope you know you're in my heart.

With appreciation and love, KI

FOREWORD

◆ ◆

I always tell people that I have the best job in the world. As a co-author, I have had the opportunity to work on many wonderful books over the years with incredibly special personalities. Each of my clients has touched my life (and the lives of millions of readers) in a unique and positive way. I was honored when Kathy Ireland suggested that I write the Foreword for her book. Usually, my clients turn to a friend, pastor, or colleague to write the Foreword. Kathy explained to me that though she could have called on someone else, she felt that I could present my personal experience of working with her in a way that might help you, the reader, to better understand the lessons that are contained throughout the following pages. This book has brought the level of my work to a new and exciting higher place, and it is my privilege to share my newfound excitement with you.

I really didn't know what to expect before my first

meeting with Kathy Ireland. I couldn't seem to understand why Kathy would be writing a book about anything other than fashion, modeling, health, home, or beauty. Once I met her face-to-face, however, the reasons for Kathy writing this book became instantly and perfectly clear to me. Sitting with Kathy, I was definitely taken by her outward beauty. She is absolutely stunning. To my surprise, as soon as she began to speak, I was captivated by the depth and certainty with which she expressed her thoughts and opinions and was even more mesmerized by Kathy's inner beauty. She is so solid in her beliefs. It only took a second to realize that Kathy Ireland is more than just a pretty face. Rarely, if ever, have I met someone who inspires me to *be* more, *do* more, *expect* more, and *give* more of myself to others. Capturing the essence of her voice has been a precious opportunity for me in my career, one for which I am truly grateful.

Kathy is certainly a world-class model. What you may not realize is that she is also a world-class humanitarian and entrepreneur. Initially, she became known for her success in the modeling industry. She has successfully made the transition from the beach to the boardroom and has created one of the most diverse and well-respected brands in America today. The vision at Kathy Ireland WorldWide was launched with a line of socks. Today, her efforts include home furnishings and flooring, which recently earned the legendary Good Housekeeping Seal, apparel, sewing patterns, home accessories, lighting, television, and publishing. In fact, the Associated Press recognized Kathy as a Best Friend to working mothers. Kathy Ireland is a wife and mother, lifestyle designer and chair and CEO of Kathy Ireland WorldWide.

Kathy carefully began building her brand, introducing new products and partnering with some of the world's successful business leaders. As a result of her hard work and dedication to quality, the Kathy Ireland brand has been recognized as the #1 brand in its category for product innovation in America, by the country's leading research firm, Kurt Salmon Associates.

As a testament to her abilities to build and operate a thriving company, Kathy has been honored by The National Association of Women Business Owners and received the Entertainment Business Woman of the Year Award. She also received the National Association of Business Leaders Award, plus she was named the Mother of the Year by the Mother's Day Association in 2002. With her outstanding business achievements, Kathy is now a sought-after speaker on how to achieve success, which is the primary content of this book.

Kathy shares her design philosophies by providing

content to magazines like *Good Housekeeping Do It Yourself*, *House Beautiful Kitchen and Baths*, *House Beautiful Remodeling and Decorating*, and *Opulence Magazine*. Even with Kathy's responsibilities caring for her family and designing and promoting her collections, she actively works with various nonprofit organizations. She is the Entertainment Industries Foundation's Ambassador for Women's Health Issues and Ambassador for the National Women's Cancer Research Alliance. She received the 2001 Jane Wyman Humanitarian Award from the Arthritis Foundation and is the chairperson of family services and parenting for Athletes and Entertainers for Kids. She is active in the Special Olympics. Kathy is responsible for the endowment of the Floyd Hall fellowship grant program, which is awarded annually by the American Paralysis Association to the leading scientist in the field of spinal cord regeneration. Because of her dedication to these and other health issues, UCLA named her as one of the Top Ten Women Health Advocates in America. And, as if that isn't enough, she also teaches Sunday school!

How's that for a short résumé? I will admit that after our first few meetings I kept thinking she's too good to be true. People warned me prior to our initial meeting that I would absolutely feel this way. I just kept waiting for a slipup. I actually thought I was a busy person until I met Kathy! Now, whenever I say that I didn't have the time for something, I realize that I simply didn't *make* the time.

Kathy has come a long way since her beginnings in Santa Barbara, California, first as a model and today as one of the few people in the world who have been able to take awareness and turn it into a worldwide brand. The Eight Powerful Inspirations that Kathy shares in this book have made her and her company among the most successful in the world, not in spite of her values and beliefs, but because of them.

The heart of this book is simple, yet truly powerful. As we wrote this book, I started to use her lessons in my own life, and they do work. Though we don't share the same religious faith, we certainly share a similar belief in the strength of God. As a strong Christian, Kathy's faith is ever present in her life. She isn't the kind of person who simply claims to be a Christian. She honestly talks the talk and walks the walk. What you see is exactly what you get from her. She truly knows her subject matter and isn't afraid to engage in dialogue with anyone about her beliefs. She is a lovely, charming, bright, and successful *role model*, and anyone who reads this book can benefit from the information she provides, regardless of their beliefs and background. She is truly gifted, and now she wants to share that gift with you. If you apply the eight inspirations that guide Kathy through her life's journey to your own life, I know you will be touched and forever changed in a wonderful, beautiful, and very powerful way.

—Laura Morton

INTRODUCTION

◈ ◈

While working on this book, the lives of people
everywhere were touched and changed forever by
the most horrific and unimaginable acts of terrorism
in the history of the United States. I was in Vermont
shooting an episode of *Home Again* with Bob Vila.
Our hearts broke as we watched the devastation
unfold. People held each other and cried. In that
moment, a group of working people became a family.
During the painful days that followed, I realized the
importance of moving forward and was humbled by
the courage and strength of the men and women who
showed unparalleled dedication in the rescue effort.
Their bravery was inspirational and the world was
awestruck by the outpouring of unity displayed by our
entire country and our friends in foreign lands. Angels
and heroes are among us. God's presence makes this
possible. With God's love, we are capable of great

things—even overcoming tremendous loss, pain, and heartache.

Countless families needlessly lost loved ones. As we each wiped tears from our disbelieving eyes, we were awakened to a new era of life in this great country of ours. My husband and I pondered what all of this meant to our family and loved ones and, though we did not lose anyone we knew personally, we grieved for the loss of life and innocence and the security we took for granted. We enjoyed a world our children will never know.

We may not always know the right thing to do in troubled times, but the overwhelming majority of us are believers in a just and loving God. This was not an act of God. We wept. We mourned. And, we rose in defense of all that we cherish. There are flashes of rage, but what ultimately overrides that is a sense of hurt for the tremendous devastation.

We can never take our families, our lives, or our freedom for granted. Every moment we have is a gift from God. That is the single most important lesson we all must learn, and then live each day so that it becomes our best. Life can change in an instant—take the time to enjoy the moment and to appreciate all of the blessings we share. Ultimately, I feel as if the tragedy on September 11 helped me to dig deeper within myself and find an even greater strengthening and belief in my faith. With God's love, I know in my heart that out of this horrific nightmare, we—each and every one of us—have emerged stronger, more united, and filled with greater hope for the future.

In light of the attacks on September 11, there was a need to take a step back and analyze why I was writing this book and what could be accomplished in doing so. I know a lot of you are going through changes in your lives, and there are many people still grieving, losing jobs, getting divorced, experiencing health challenges, or facing financial problems. This book will help you manage and navigate through any crisis. Being asked to write this book is such a tremendous honor, particularly because one of my earlier job descriptions was to simply "shut up and pose." Though modeling was not something that I aspired to, I'm extremely grateful for the opportunities and education it provided me. It exposed me to the best designers in the world. It exposed me to people of different cultures so I could learn how they live and what it is that they need. It also alerted me to images and prices that are not realistic. I always knew that when I had my own brand I wanted it to be for real women. Public speaking and writing are not things I dreamed would be part of my career. A critic once wrote that I had a voice that could kill small animals. That critic would probably have been equally impressed by my initial efforts in putting my thoughts about this book on paper.

Even though Doubleday asked me to write this book, I still had questions about what it was that I had to offer you. I've been blessed with the support of the millions of women who believe in my brand. For everybody else, if you're even familiar with me at all, you might know me as that model person. You may be asking yourself, "What's she going to do? Teach me a new pose?" Okay. If you're interested. After a big meal, if you turn sideways and then twist your upper body, you can give the illusion of a waist. After a really big meal, you get a really good photo retoucher! Mine is a woman named Paulinda . . . that's the biggest secret of modeling.

Some of you may think of me as a spokesperson who lends my name and does endorsements. Maybe you think the people liked my poses, so they paid me a bunch of money to take pictures and show up at glamorous events. Would you enter into a long-term strategic partnership with someone on whom your profits depended because you liked her poses? I didn't think so. The teams of all the companies I work with feel the same way.

The eight lessons in this book have literally changed my life. But why would that be interesting to you? I can be so bold as to say these powerful inspirations and lessons will change your life, because they don't come from me. *Your* inspirations that support each lesson come from God. When you apply them to your life, *your life will change*.

Success comes from learning, from gathering information from the best sources available. I have been blessed to meet and work with some incredible people—people who are geniuses in the truest sense of the word, like First Lady Laura Bush, Anthony Robbins, Paul Newman, Martha Williamson, who produces *Touched by an Angel*, Bill Cosby, and Jule Campell, formerly of Time/Warner, who produced the best photography during my days of working with *Sports Illustrated*, Jaclyn Smith, who pioneered people developing their own retail brands rather than endorsing for others, and Eunice Kennedy Shriver, who founded the Special Olympics. Jule, Jaclyn, and Ms. Kennedy Shriver are three wonderful women whose friendship I cherish and are mentors to me. If you allow yourself the opportunity, *you can be mentored by someone you've never met*. For me, one of those people would be Carol Black, the CEO of Lifetime Television. Although I know nothing about her personal life, in business I have learned so much from watching how she brilliantly built her career by serving women. She teaches by example. I try to do that.

In my life, I surround myself with people I respect.

I listen to them, and ultimately I make up my own mind as to whether their information is something that makes sense to me. I either apply it or eject it from my brain. Success is a give-and-take situation. Whenever you're learning you are taking. I have always been a taker. I am ready to absorb whatever information will benefit my life and my work. I plan to continue taking, because I never want to stop learning. I now realize that it is also time for me to become a giver and share whatever I have learned. If there's one piece of information here that you can use, I will be happy.

It's certainly not that I have all the answers. In fact, after you've finished this book, you might want to eject everything you've read from your brain. Perhaps you'll want to have a word with me afterward. Please do. Contact me at kathyireland.com. I would love to hear your thoughts. I don't sell anything on my website. It is strictly an opportunity for me to communicate with people. I thrive on feedback. That's how I learn. That's how I grow.

Something that I know and I love about each of you without knowing you personally is that you're all risk-takers. I love, respect, and know that with the demands on everyone's time and resources today, picking up this book is taking a risk and making an investment. While we all have different backgrounds and different circumstances, I'm sure that there is a lot that we all have in common. Whether you drive a bus, are a stay-at-home mom, or run a company, *you* are the CEO and entrepreneur of your life. Today, corporations, churches, and organizations throughout our country ask me to speak with people about my journey from the beach to the boardroom. Well here it is. . . .

How many of you worked as children? See, we do have a lot in common. My first job began when I was four years old. I painted rocks and sold them from my wagon. These rocks were multi-functional. Not only were they *objets d'art* (I am still working on the pronunciation) very beautiful on any cocktail table, they also served as paperweights. My granny carried them in her purse at all times along with her knitting needles as a means of self-defense. This was before the days of mace. My sister Mary and I did this business venture together. Mary, being three years older and having more experience than me, sold her rocks for ten cents each, and I sold mine for five cents each. Even though mine were sold less expensively, I did really well. I could work very quickly and still turn out beautiful rocks. My customers really appreciated the value. From early on, I understood that I needed to give people the best possible product for their money.

From painting rocks, I went on to watering plants.

If I knew then what I know now, I would've done things a lot differently. I would've enlisted a buddy and delegated some of those duties. I had a great vision of how I wanted those gardens to look, but I didn't have the skill set to back me up. I have to admit that I killed more than a few plants. So I was out of work and on to the next project, which was washing cars. I didn't really love that. I was waiting for my life's work—a paper route. Where I grew up, you had to be eleven and a half to have your own route. I just knew that was the job for me. I used to pester the boy who had the route before me. I'd ask him if I could help fold and deliver the papers. I'd try to tag along and learn the ropes so that I would be prepared when my day came. Even then, I knew the importance of having a plan. I was going to be ready. Shortly before I came of age, my father showed me an ad in the newspaper offering a paper-route opportunity. Great! Except for one thing. The ad asked, "Are you the boy for the job?"

My parents raised their three daughters with a total sense of male/female equality. So when he showed me the paper, Dad knew what kind of reaction the ad was going to get out of me. I wrote to the editor and I said, "No, I'm not the boy for the job, I'm the girl for the job, and I can do it just as well as any boy. I think that I deserve a chance."

My first day on the job was New Year's Day. The newspaper was extra big and heavier than usual. I was a very skinny kid, and I remember thinking I didn't know what I had gotten myself into. The papers were so big that when I loaded up my sacks, I couldn't lift them to put them on. I had to crawl on my belly and stick my head through and then stand up. I had another sack loaded onto my bicycle and, as I was riding along and getting rid of the papers in the front, the sack would fly up and choke me, and I'd fall over. I had one customer who I'll never forget. I was riding up the hill, and the gentleman stopped me and said "What are you doing here? You have no business doing this. It is a boy's job, and you'll never last." I didn't let him see me cry, and to this day I'm very grateful to him, because he made me stick it out when I wanted to quit. For three years in a row, I was nominated as carrier of the year, and I won each year for my district. I still thank that man for his inspiration.

I am very thankful that my dad taught me the importance of a solid work ethic at a very young age. He would say things to me like "Kathy, if your customers expect their paper on their driveway, put it on their porch." That was the foundation of my learning to under-promise and over-deliver. From the day I got my route, I committed to deliver papers to my customers better than they had ever been delivered before. Always give 110 percent. We try to practice that philosophy in daily living and at my company, Kathy Ireland WorldWide. My paper route taught me a lot about business and even more about life. Twenty-seven years later, I'm still that girl with the paper route.

You are probably wondering what is Kathy Ireland WorldWide? My company's mission is to find solutions for families, especially busy moms. It was never my ambition to become a model, and I have never understood the term supermodel. It's not like being a superhero! I was a gawky kid with one thick eyebrow, and attractive was never a word I would use when I looked at myself in the mirror. Growing up, I dreamed of being a reporter because of my thirst for knowledge, a marine biologist because of my love of the ocean, or a teacher because of my love for children. In some ways, I am fulfilling my dream of teaching in my business career. My Sunday school teachings, my health and wellness videos, and my fashion and home designs have all offered the opportunity to share knowledge with others. My design career was launched with socks. My friends and partners, John and Marilyn Moretz, are the best sock manufacturers in America. Long before it was commonplace, we made surprise factory inspections at Moretz Mills to be comfortable with the working conditions there.

Next, we tested out those socks and loved them. We loaded up our backpacks and went around the country presenting socks to retailers. With my modeling background, beginning a brand with swimsuits would have been too obvious for me. I believed if women embraced my socks, we might have something.

I like starting from the ground up. We had very few resources, no advertising budget—just a dream, good products, good partners, and hard work. Women loved our socks, and that is how it all began. Today, our efforts include apparel, jewelry, home furnishings, flooring, lighting, home accessories, wall art, housewares, mattresses, window coverings, outdoor living, food and entertainment, television, publishing, and home design services. When I speak around the country, or stand on line at the grocery store, the people who are aware of my business ask how we are able to accomplish what we do—especially since my priorities are my faith and my family.

I work hard to stay grounded in the reality of every situation that I face. Whether you are leading a company or managing the latest family dilemma, you need entrepreneurial spirit. You must perform a constant dance between the dream of your vision and the reality you are experiencing. It is easy to become so rooted in reality that you abandon your dream. Life becomes gray, and the passion that once ignited and excited you is lost. Similarly, it's equally possible to become so intoxicated by your dream that reality sneaks away, and what you want to happen never does. You need to acknowledge reality and dreams with the same veracity. What I've learned from successful entrepreneurs is to take reality in one hand and the dream in the other and allow them both to drive and inspire the vision you have for your life.

There is a huge cavern between imagination and implementation. No one person can do everything all of the time. You can't let the idea of not doing everything on your own stop you from your dreams. You need to learn to ask for help, to accept that help, and then take action. Never be afraid to ask for help. What I hope to show people in this book is how true success comes from knowing and accepting God and understanding that He loves you for who you are regardless of your flaws. This kind of success is attainable to everyone. A person who doesn't share my faith can still benefit from what's written in this book. Because the inspirations are from God, they are meant for each and every person. My faith is critical to choices I make every day. But, even with the strongest faith, you still have to know and understand how to make good decisions, and that's the cornerstone of these eight powerful lessons and the scriptures that inspire them. Each is *powerful* (definition: influential, commanding, authoritative, controlling, prevailing, dominant, potent, and great!) and has helped me to grow, inspire, educate, and handle the challenges we all face in everyday life.

May God bless you and your loved ones in the days ahead.

Love,
Kathy

Chapter One

POWERFUL
INSPIRATIONS

❖   ❖

Inspiration

ALL THINGS ARE POSSIBLE
WITH GOD.

Mark 10:27

I don't remember a time in my life when I didn't believe in God. My faith came in stages. As a young child, there were a few years when my family went to church. Ironically, the church we attended didn't have Bibles. There were some books that had excerpts from the Bible, but I always had questions. Who put those selected passages together? Where were the rest of the scriptures? The message was delivered in an angry tone with a very thick accent. I never quite understood anything that was being said, but I remember feeling guilty, scared, and like I could never measure up. The whole experience felt kind of cold. I never felt any love in that particular congregation. I am sure that same feeling can be found in any place of worship for any faith. My earliest recollection of church was that it didn't feel like a happy place—it was just something that I had to do.

The God I knew from that church seemed unkind

to me. I didn't really like Him. I was scared of God when I was a child. Maybe it was the way in which the message was delivered, but something about that whole experience really frightened me. I was a little confused about the experience. I think my family may have felt the same way because eventually we all stopped going to church. Nobody ever seemed to have the answers for my questions. When it came time for me to go to church, I didn't want to go. I didn't understand why I couldn't talk directly to the Big Guy myself instead of through a middleman. I didn't get it. My mom told me some people believe that religious leaders are on a different level than regular humans. Hmmm. They're closer to God, and we need them to translate for us. Mom and I had a hard time understanding that belief.

As I grew older, I still believed in God, but He wasn't a big part of my life. I always felt like there were two Gods—the God I knew in my head who I loved and the God from church who I didn't much care for. I continued to pray on my own, if only in my head. That God was great. I had some prayers answered the way I wanted them answered, and that made me so happy. The God I prayed to was like a friend—like my buddy. He was always there when I needed Him. I wish I could say that I was always there for Him, but I know I wasn't. I found out that God is

not this big killjoy. It took me a long time to understand that God wants to keep us from pain, not
pleasure. When I became a teenager, I really began to
put my faith and God on the back shelf. I was totally
self-absorbed, and the idea of making time for God
seemed like a waste to me.

I remember regularly sitting in my Spanish class,
being really mad at God. I should have been studying,
but instead I was pouting. I was upset with God
for making me so dorky. I was in a very awkward
phase. I was tall and skinny so my pants were always
too short. I wore pigtails, and when I cut them off
my hair poufed up big. My family didn't know
about conditioner—something I would discover later.
I couldn't understand why I didn't fit in and why I
didn't have any friends. The girl who had the locker
next to mine would kick me on my way to class. Kids
made fun of me all the time. I didn't like being different, and I wallowed in teenage angst and self-pity. I
would have done anything to fit in with the other
kids. I was so tired of feeling alone and lonely. I would
have hung out with the most troubled kids just to do
whatever it took to have a sense of belonging and
acceptance. I remember thinking that I would have
slept with boys or taken drugs if it meant someone
would like me.

In retrospect, I am very thankful that God made

me geeky so that doing those things was never really an option. Even the kids who were troublemakers didn't want to be my friends! As I sat there in Spanish class one day, staring out at the clouds, I was pretty desperate. I made a decision to take a leap. It was time to trust and believe that God loved me. *He made me, and he doesn't make mistakes.* I realized that being different was a good thing. Suddenly, making fun of me became like making fun of Him, and that didn't seem right. Physically, I still looked the same, but losing my desperation for acceptance made me more attractive to others, and soon I made my first friend, Jenny, who is still one of my best friends. To this day, the knowledge that God loves me is the greatest source of my self-esteem. It's not from any of my accomplishments—it's from God.

I was "discovered" at Betty Mazetti's LaBelles's Modeling School by an agent from the Elite modeling agency. I didn't want to pursue modeling, but I knew in my heart that I had to check it out. I didn't want to wonder about what might have been the rest of my life. I spent a summer in New York trying to get work and, immediately after graduating from high school, while my friends headed off to enjoy their Disneyland graduation trip, I was on a plane to Rome for my first international job. Instead of being excited about the adventure, I was drowning in self-pity because I couldn't spend the summer on the beach now that I finally had friends.

Becoming a model was such a surprise career, and it was a very confusing time for me. I decided I'd try it out for six months, take the money, and run. I traveled to countries where I didn't speak the language, I didn't know anyone, and it was a really crazy time in the fashion business. There were lots of activities around me like drugs, casual sex, and all kinds of manipulation. It was a world I simply wasn't used to, and it was terribly lonely.

My next international trip was to Paris. I was eighteen years old. I stayed at the apartment of someone I worked with. I had a room that was at the end of a long hallway, which later on other girls told me they referred to as the dungeon. Someone who lived in the house was less than discreet with his sexual overtures, and I never felt very safe. My memories of Paris are of going straight to my room and locking my door.

Before I left home, my mother had packed a Bible in my suitcase, and it was out of sheer boredom and loneliness that I picked it up and started reading. As I began to read the Bible, I started with the Gospels, and I found that I couldn't put it down. I was riveted as I read all about Jesus. I thought, Wow, He's really cool. He's not anything like I thought. I became a Christian when I was eighteen years old. Reading about Jesus was incredible. He was nothing like I imagined. He wasn't out there judging everyone and condemning everyone. He was loving and leading. What I learned that day of His unconditional love forever changed my life and my perspective on everything. I knew that if He was with me, who could be against me?

My friendship with Jesus prepared me and gave me the strength to never compromise my character to achieve any goal. Shortly after arriving in Paris, I was doing a photo shoot, and the photographer asked me to take my shirt off. I told him that I wouldn't do that because I didn't feel comfortable. I don't judge other women who make that choice. A lot of the women I worked with grew up in Europe, where nudity is more common and no big deal. I grew up in Southern California, where you can get arrested for such things. I'm a bit of a prude. He tried everything to convince me to take my top off. He showed me stacks of magazines of women who were successful who had. I told him to get one of them to do the photo. It wasn't for me. He became very pushy and crossed the line, actually physically pushing me. I'm not a violent person, but I had to physically push him back, and I walked off the job.

My newfound strength knowing that God was with me and that it didn't matter what anyone else thought got me through that experience and so many other challenges along the way. The photographer told me that I would never make it in the business if I didn't take my top off. He was so wrong. I didn't have to compromise to have a career. I learned that all things are possible with God, and that helps me in my personal life and in my career today.

As I continued to read the Bible, I discovered how Jesus loved people—especially women. As a young woman out in the world, in a business that felt dominated by men, I was very frustrated. I knew that women had challenges in my own country, but as I traveled to other countries and experienced firsthand how women were often treated, it was very hard for me to comprehend. What I learned about Jesus was how much He loves, respects, and honors all women, and He did this during biblical times, when we were not even considered *second-class* citizens. It's important to remember that God chose a woman to give birth to His son. The first person that Jesus told that He was the Son of God was a woman. She was a Samaritan, and at that time, Jews did not speak to Samaritans. Men did not speak to women, let alone a woman who was leading what was considered an immoral life. Jesus loved her and though He didn't

condone her sins, He didn't stand in judgment of
them. He acknowledged them in a loving way, and He
chose her because He had respect for her in spite of
her sins.

The first people that Jesus appeared to when He
arose from the dead were women. To me, that was
so encouraging. He became my best friend, and I suddenly was no longer lonely. No matter where I was,
I knew that He would be with me. I often wondered
why God put me in the modeling business. Today, I
believe that it was because He knew me. I had such a
rebellious nature. If I had been in a healthier profession, I might have turned against the good things and
destroyed genuine opportunities. As it was, I was
rejecting a lot of things that would have been less
than good for me. I refused to become a victim of all
the negativity that was so easily and readily accessible. For the first time in my life, I *wanted* to be
different. Those junior high–school rejections were
now serving me well. I didn't want to fit in with the
crowd. I didn't want that lifestyle. In retrospect, it
was a healthy rebellion. I refused to go to certain parties. I tried to avoid situations with people I couldn't
trust. Watching people do things that were making
them unhappy and unhealthy reminded me of how I
felt back in school—wanting to fit in and watching

everyone else wanting to fit in and be like everyone else. When exactly do we get over that need?

My walk with the Lord continued at a very slow pace after I began reading the Bible in Paris. I am a slow and deliberate learner, and I remained a baby Christian for a very long time. I still feel like a baby Christian, but I was an infant due to my own hesitations in following His word.

As I read the Bible, I would kind of pick and choose passages that I liked and try to live by those words. On the other hand, I'd get to certain parts of the Bible and I was positive that what I was reading had to be a typo or incorrect in some way because it made no sense to me at all. So I cherry-picked the passages that meant something to me and abandoned the parts of the Bible that I didn't relate to. Eventually, I realized that what I was doing was trying to mold God into what I wanted Him to be, rather than letting Him mold me into the person He created me to be. My lack of obedience made my life so much harder than it needed to be. I made too many mistakes along the way that could have been avoided if I had simply obeyed God's word. I've been humbled many, many times. I understand that God wants us to share a joy and a fellowship that we all need. It saddens me when I see other people making the same mistakes that I've made—mistakes like waiting to be happy when you have the choice to be happy today or blaming other people for circumstances in your life. A close friend of mine often says, "In relationships, there are no victims, only volunteers." I believe that. I also know that developing character is a path that is never completed. It's not a destination.

As I continued my Christian walk, I was inspired by something I read by C. S. Lewis. It said that it was impossible for Jesus to simply be a "good man." He could be only one of three things. First, He could be a very evil man, because He told everyone that He was the Son of God and He told people to follow Him and allowed His followers to die for Him. If He did that and it was not true, then He was indeed a very evil man. Second, He was simply crazy, because He thought that He was the Son of God, but He wasn't. That leaves the final thing that Jesus could be, and that is exactly who He says He was. That is what I know in my heart. I am so encouraged by that belief. He knows me for who I am and hears all of my thoughts, and yet . . . He still loves me. Now that I know Him, it is so hard to imagine that this man died for me—for all of us. His desire is that not one of us should perish, but that we should all be with Him forever. He thought enough of us to give us free will, that we can choose to love Him or not, but He is always there for us with open arms, loving us. If I have a question or a concern or a challenge, I pray about it. I ask for guidance, help, and answers. Faith is courage that has said its prayers. Jesus Christ is my Lord and Savior and I place my faith in Him. I am confident in the possibilities that are present in all of our lives.

If I don't feel at peace about something, then it's not God's will. Every day I ask God that His will be done in my life, which isn't always easy for someone like me, who likes to be in control. The Bible is the greatest book ever written for managing life. The basis for all the information we seek and need to know is right there—available to anyone who reads God's word.

Faith is a lifetime journey. Through years of study, prayer, and practical experience, I now understand that I truly want God to be in charge of all things, because He has a greater sense of the "big picture" than I ever could understand. I recognize that sometimes His path isn't the path I'd choose or the easiest road to travel, but it is always the path I need to be on in order to grow and fully enrich my life and the lives of those around me.

I am a bit of a control freak, so asking that God's will be done over my own is, in itself, a daily challenge for me. When I give up that control and accept that He is truly in charge of all things, I am at peace.

I trust Him even though I know it doesn't always mean that everything is going to be easy. Life is tough, and you have to be, too. Every day we live is filled with uncertainty. As people of God, we don't know what tomorrow holds, but we know who holds tomorrow. God can make the impossible possible. My prayer for each one of you is simple. If you don't know Jesus Christ, that you take the time to get to know Him. Invest the time in a relationship with Him. He will bless you more than you can imagine.

LESSON ONE

Faith is the key to stability and the cornerstone of life.

- Life is tough. Faith will get you through the tough times.

- When God is with us, who can be against us?

- Never compromise your character to achieve any goal.

- Faith takes courage and is rewarded.

- Character is a path, not a destination.

- Faith is everlasting.

- The Bible is the greatest book ever written for managing life.

Chapter Two

POWERFUL YOU

❖ ❖

Inspiration

LET US RUN WITH PERSEVERANCE
THE RACE MARKED OUT FOR US.

Hebrews 12:1

As a child I watched a lot of TV, and you know what? I realized that I didn't want to just *watch* other people having lives . . . I wanted to have a life, too. I want to live life to the fullest. What's the use of just being a spectator and standing on the sidelines watching life go by? God gave each of us so many unique abilities. We have to take responsibility and be active to have fuller, richer, happier lives. How many of you have been told you shouldn't, you can't, you're not good enough, you're not smart enough? I certainly have, and please don't let it stop you from trying.

At age sixteen my parents gave me a gift of a course in modeling. My mom told me that she felt guilty that I never had "lessons" as a kid. I took ballet one afternoon, but I didn't like it, so I never went back. I was kind of a tomboy. I was always burping. Mom thought a modeling class might help me become more of a lady. I had the opportunity to take a wonderful modeling course from Betty Mazetti-Hatch's school. She still lives in Santa Barbara. The course taught us how to look a certain way and showed us how to correct certain "flaws" by deemphasizing some features and highlighting others. It was a magician's course in Grooming Illusion 101. The school gave us an honest introduction to the real world of modeling. Although there were great benefits for me from the course and the profession, modeling schools and the work itself are something I usually never recommend. Even then, I couldn't help but wonder who in the fashion world made up this version of the "right" or "wrong" way to look. I've always liked the idea of taking what you have and enhancing it, while camouflaging whatever *you're* not comfortable with. In my case, you already know that I have one long thick eyebrow. I learned that plucking gives the illusion of two separate eyebrows and I think that it's an illusion that works *for* me.

After being "discovered," I lived in New York for part of the summer. My agents explained to my parents that they would advance the money for me to be able to live in one of their "models" apartments. If I was unhappy for any reason, I would be able to leave. As much as I didn't want to go, I knew that if I didn't explore this opportunity I might regret it. Mom agreed to go to New York with me for the first five days.

The first morning I showed up at my agency, I had this image in my mind of what I was supposed to look like. I bought a fancy outfit and a pair of "Candies" with high spiky heels—something I never wore growing up. I was a beach rat—I owned one pair of flip-flops. In the winter, I wore socks with them. I was trying so hard to be who I thought the agency wanted me to be, and in the process I was completely untrue to myself. The blisters from the heels? Just a bonus.

I lived in the apartment with several other girls from the same agency. Most of them were younger than me. We all came from different parts of the country and from different sets of circumstances. One girl was very elegant, and she was always tidying up. I, of course, was a total slob. Another girl always walked in front of everyone else. Another girl was really fun. She loved adventure. For one girl modeling was everything. Another girl had a really great sense of humor. There were two rules in the apartment—no cigarettes or boys—but that didn't address the drugs that came in the mail. It was an eclectic mix to say the least, but they were really great girls. We bonded and became like sisters. I learned to celebrate our differences, and somehow that made it work.

Two weeks after getting to New York, the owner

of the agency called me up and said, "Congratula-
tions, Kathy! You've got your first job, and it's with a
good friend of mine!" He went on and on about how
great this photographer was to work with and how I
wouldn't have to worry about a thing. I thought to
myself, this is going to be great. I won't have to worry
about this being a legitimate situation because the
photographer was the owner's friend. I was told that it
was a photo test for *Modern Bride*. A photo test is like
an audition for new models. We were shooting out of
town on a Saturday. I was supposed to return to Manhattan that night, and then the shoot was supposed to
be on Monday. The photographer came into the city
to pick me up. I had my makeup and hairbrush with
me and not a dime in my pocket. I figured we'd be
back in a few hours.

The whole drive out, I kept getting this weird
feeling from the photographer. He gave me the creeps,
but I just kept telling myself that he was the owner's
friend and that maybe it was because he was Euro-
pean—I still hadn't gotten used to the kisses on the
cheeks. I asked him what time we'd be back that
night, and he said he must have forgotten to tell me,
but he decided it was too much of a hassle to drive
back and forth to Manhattan, so he got us a hotel
room. Of course, there was only one room and only
one bed—which he told me I could have as long as he

could come snuggle with me in the middle of the night! I was completely freaked out. All I could think of was whether or not I should jump out of the car as he was speeding down the highway!

We got to the hotel, and thankfully it was still daylight. I ran to the phone and called my roommates, reversing the charges to my home phone. I didn't even have a dime for the call, which taught me a valuable lesson that is always to have what I call a "security fund" when I traveled, meaning having enough money for a taxi home. Because the photographer was right there, I tried to speak to them in code, but wasn't making very much sense. When my roommates asked, "How's it going?" I said, "No." They guessed the problem and she said they would send my good friend Lloyd to get me. (He was always so wonderful to me.) We actually did the photos. I knew it would be at least two hours before Lloyd got there and I felt it would be safe doing the test shoot in daylight on a busy beach. Afterward, I went back to the hotel and waited for Lloyd. The photographer was unaware of my escape plan. I got on the phone with a friend from Santa Barbara. It was another reversed charge call— which by the way I found later when I got my phone bill, is very expensive. Somehow being on the phone made me feel safe—like I wasn't alone in the room with him. He lay down on the bed and started snoring away. I could see his eyes slightly open—barely squinting. He was faking! I got out of there so fast. I went to the lobby and waited for my ride.

I felt so humiliated that I had gotten myself into that situation. I was embarrassed for not knowing better and mad at myself that it happened. All I wanted to do was go home—back to California. Lloyd, who treated my roommates and me like he was our big brother, picked me up and took me to a friend's house. She was an adult who was very kind. She seemed sophisticated and had friends visiting. She told me to make myself at home. I was so embarrassed about my situation. I went to sleep and got up early the next morning. I grabbed a cookie from the kitchen and started walking. Due to distractions during high-school geography class, I thought if I followed the coastline, it would eventually get me back to Santa Barbara. I forgot about South America. As I walked, I was getting angrier and angrier because I really wanted that job. I was supposed to be paid $300 a day, which is still a lot of money to me. It seemed so unfair that because this photographer was a total jerk, I wasn't going to get to do the job.

As I tried to make my way back to California via Long Island, a car pulled over and asked if I was okay. I probably looked a little out of place wandering by myself. The driver and passenger were older guys, and my awakening instincts told me they were safe, perhaps genuinely concerned for me. I asked if they would give me a lift back to the hotel. Somehow, I found an inner strength that gave me the ability to go back and confront this guy. I walked up, looked him square in the eyes, and said, "I want to do this job, and we're going to do the job I was hired for without having to sleep with you. Don't even think about messing around with me." And that was that.

On the day of the photo shoot, I told the editor from the magazine what had happened. She seemed shocked because he had told them that I was his girlfriend and that they didn't need to pay for two rooms, since the budget was so tight for the shoot.

When I got back to New York City, I confronted the owner about what had happened. It felt like a visit to the principal's office. I was seventeen years old, and the owner of the agency was telling me that I was overreacting and that if his friend hadn't been so clumsy, maybe things would have worked out a little better. . . . I couldn't believe how impaired his judgment was. I tried to explain to him that there were younger girls at the agency, twelve- and thirteen-year-old girls who might not be able to get away from a terrible situation. I was assured that this

photographer wouldn't be allowed to work with any of
the girls anymore. I later learned that lasted only for
the summer I was in New York.

From that experience, I realized modeling was
going to present a set of challenges I had never
encountered before. In spite of that, I wanted to pursue the opportunity. I needed to know if I could
conquer the challenges.

After that summer, I decided to go back to Santa
Barbara, get my old job back as the hostess of Petrini's
Restaurant, and be with my friends. While I did
meet some people in the modeling business that
were unsavory, I also had the opportunity to meet
some incredible people who helped change my life
in the most positive ways. One of those people is a
man named Frankie Mayer, who is a designer, stylist,
editor, literally a master of many trades. If it weren't
for Frankie, I would never have gone off to Europe.
He arranged to have me flown over to work with
Peter Lindburgh, who was and is one of the world's
finest photographers. Frankie always made sure everything was going to be okay and that I'd never have to
worry about finding myself in an awkward situation
like I had in New York, although I always remained
on guard. Frankie took care of everything and gave
my parents and me reassurance that I was in good
hands.

◈ ◈

Up until my late twenties, I had extremely bad eyesight. That inability to see clearly became one of my coping mechanisms over the years. It gave me a nice, fuzzy little world. I could only see whatever was right in front of me. In a way, my blurry vision was like my own version of escapism because I didn't have to deal with things if I didn't want to. I could choose to be oblivious to everything going on around me.

I used that fuzzy world as protective armor so that I didn't have to connect with the aspects of life that I found so miserable. I was constantly away from home, and all I could think of while traveling was how much I missed my family and friends. I didn't take the opportunity to explore any of the places I visited. I missed out on the architecture and culture on those early trips because I was so lonely. Meeting new people felt like a waste of time and energy because I thought I would never see any of them again, so what was the point? I knew that modeling wasn't going to be a long-term goal. I was always planning on moving into something else very soon. Eventually I realized what a selfish loser I was being.

I made a conscious decision to try and become friends with new people I met on jobs. I was determined to make the most out of each situation. I made a fool out of myself regularly. At least I was breaking out of that cold shell I used to hide in. Once, on an

Avon catalogue job, there were some stylists who were obsessed with fashion, talking about this designer and that designer, who was in and who was out. I never much cared about haute couture (which years later I learned meant "high fashion"), but in an effort to become friends I tried to join their conversation. After all, I figured that maybe they were missing their friends and family, too, and I wanted to give it a try. I heard them talking about Yom Kippur this and Yom Kippur that. I asked if Yom Kippur was a new Japanese designer. The women stared at me in complete disbelief. I had no idea they were speaking about one of the most sacred Jewish holidays. We did not become buddies on that job.

In a strange way, my awful eyesight gave me the ability to not have to see things clearly. While doing the film *Necessary Roughness*, I started wearing contact lenses to develop better foot-eye coordination because I had to learn to kick a football. The character I was playing was a kicker on a college team. I got pretty good. In fact, I entertained the fantasy of turning pro, but I was quickly humbled by the reality of my limitations. Getting those contact lenses didn't actually open my eyes for the first time, but they certainly coincided with my new clearer vision for my future. The funny thing is, I liked the idea of knowing that if I wanted to, I could take the lenses out. It was like a little crutch that I had whenever I didn't want to see the world or certain situations perfectly clear. I had so many embarrassing moments when I didn't wear the lenses. My husband and I like to go surfing in the mornings. Surfing is very territorial, and it's not a good idea to get too close to other people. I was always invading people's spaces searching for my husband. I'd paddle my way over and check out the guys carefully to be sure that I didn't start to nuzzle and cuddle with the wrong guy. It's a miracle that I never really got myself into trouble.

A few years ago, I finally had corrective eye surgery so I no longer wear contact lenses. The first time I looked in the mirror after the surgery was a bit of an adjustment for me. I looked a lot older than I thought. I noticed how dark the roots were in my hair. Little things that I hadn't really seen before or that didn't really appear visible to me were now right there in all their glory for me to see with perfect 20/20 vision!

You might say that I really saw myself—maybe for the first time in my adult life. Up until that moment I had been retouched without my lenses. After a period of adjustment, I felt comfortable with the real me. I have earned every wrinkle. I wear them with honor. As long as I have more laugh lines than frown wrinkles, I'm happy.

I suddenly became much more alert and aware of *everything* around me—especially things I had been able to effectively ignore for so many years. With my newfound vision came a sharpened ability to see things in a new way—as they really are. I started noticing behavior, others' as well as my own, that was no longer acceptable.

I was with the Elite agency on both coasts for twelve years, and even though I had enjoyed success, I believed it was time for me to move on. I decided to leave Elite because I wanted to explore opportunities outside of modeling. From the beginning of my career, Valerie Trott, my agent in the L.A. office, was very maternal, protective, concerned about me. I will always be grateful to her for that. I am a person who values loyalty—it's extremely important. I agonized over the decision to leave Elite. I never wanted to be a quitter, especially after people had invested so much time and energy in my work. I never want to let anyone down. Still, in order to persevere, I needed to work with people who saw where I was as a beginning, rather than hanging on for the "few good years" that I might have left. I didn't leave Elite for another agency. I simply left the business of being a model for hire. I wasn't happy with any aspect of the work. I wanted to develop my own business. My husband, Greg, is an emergency room physician. He'd come home, and we'd talk about him saving someone's life. I'd talk about an idea I came up with for a new pose that day. It wasn't fulfilling, and I knew in my heart that it was time to move on. I could now see things in a new way.

I never felt comfortable earning my living from how other people perceived that I looked. When asked, I almost always discourage anyone from getting into modeling. I've always felt this way about any job that chips away at someone's self-esteem. Modeling usually represents an unattainable look that few people have naturally. I've seen models starve themselves or have surgery to attain a certain type of look that they hoped would get them work. They get bulimic and anorexic. All of this damage just to get a job. Trends change, the look changes, and, suddenly, they are out of work again. Their look is no longer in fashion, and these young, wonderful people become disillusioned with life before their life has really begun. In the long run, it's not worth it. I always figured if they liked me for who I am, fine. If not, I'll do something else for a living.

I would rather lose a job than lose my self-esteem. During my *Sports Illustrated* shoots or any other shoots, I had certain rules that had to be adhered to. Suits that were too revealing were nixed. Some people thought my choices were inappropriate. Some thought my choices were prudish. Everyone has an opinion, and you have to keep that in perspective. It's just their opinion. A willingness to live in my beliefs is a part of every facet of my life. People question me often about the dichotomy between my beliefs and my career. Being a Christian and modeling bathing suits never felt strange or like anything I should be ashamed of. It felt normal to me. Having grown up on the beaches of California, being in a bathing suit was second nature. I never had any issues posing in them, as long as the client and the photographer abided by my rules.

I always struggled with the concept of anyone tying their self-worth to their outward appearance. There have been many times in my life when I felt I was being judged, initially as an awkward teenager and later as a model. It is easy for me to understand how people can turn to destructive behavior in order to gain acceptance. I see young girls struggle today with the image of how they are supposed to look. Models are being photographed at a much earlier age, some starting as young as ten years old and even younger. The messages being sent to all of these young people concern me.

As time went on, I was working so hard to improve my attitude that I tried to turn the experiences of traveling to these faraway locations into memorable and positive encounters. What was the

point of being in these places if I couldn't enjoy seeing anything? Whenever I'd travel for a shoot to a
place that I was excited about, I would try to add a few
days to my trip and wander about on my days off and
meet the local people. I loved meeting strangers in
distant places like Africa, the South Pacific, and
Brazil. I was so taken by the architecture in Rome. My
husband, Greg, met up with me on several trips. We
surfed in Indonesia and spent a romantic night in a
castle in Portugal. We drove through the Spanish
countryside. The cobblestone streets along the Seine
in Paris were especially appealing. I had to change my
perspective to fully understand what a blessing it was
to have the opportunities presented to me as a model.

From the outside looking in, how could I ever
have complained about my life and my job? Only my
closest friends understood that modeling wasn't a cool
thing for me. They knew it was a difficult time for me
and supported me through it. It was really helpful
having good friends to come home to. To cheer me
up, they'd often send me things I couldn't get in
Europe like chocolate-chip cookie dough. The people
who weren't that close to me perceived modeling as
glamorous and thought how lucky I was to travel to all
those exotic places. My life seemed exciting, and
on so many levels it was interesting, but it certainly
wasn't all roses. I started to change my attitude and

made a conscious decision to try and enjoy the ride. Making that choice helped everything change around me. I started to find the good in every single day and in that quest, I started to uncover and realize my own inner strength. I discovered something wonderful . . . a powerful me. We all have that power inside of us. It's one of God's innumerable gifts to each individual. Many of us fear tapping that power because it will certainly bring changes to your life that we may or may not be prepared to handle. Sometimes without knowing it, people who love us resist our desire to change because it can be very scary to them.

Over the years, I developed enough confidence to feel good about myself through my faith and my belief that God loves me for exactly the person that I am— flaws and all. It took time and challenges to get me to an understanding of the value of true self-worth. Placing your sense of self-worth on something that is temporary, such as your appearance, social situation, career, and even your health, is really dangerous. No one can guarantee that those things will still be in your life tomorrow. The term self-esteem can be con- fusing because it implies that it comes from us. I believe that if self-esteem comes from those tempo- rary areas, we will inevitably be disappointed. Life can change in an instant, and you better see yourself as

◇ ◇

valuable on the inside. That will sustain you in the long run.

A few days after giving a speech on self-esteem and faith, I was in our driveway playing with our son, Erik. He had just come home from school, and I had been looking forward to having a fun afternoon with him. We played a little basketball and hung out. My husband, Greg, hopped on top of Erik's wagon and was riding it like it was a skateboard. It looked like so much fun, I wanted to give it a try. I told Greg to push me, I was holding on while steering with the handle. It was sort of like wagon-surfing. He was pushing me around our driveway. It was so much fun. As we approached my parked car, I over-corrected my turn and ended up doing a face plant right on our brick driveway. I smashed my face, hurt my shoulder, bashed and broke my nose, and tore the skin away from my face. I broke some of my teeth, had a fat lip, and split my forehead open. It really hurt! All I could think was Oww!

I've never seen my husband react like he did at that moment. There was blood all over, and he had a panicked look. He took his shirt off to stop the bleeding, and he got me a towel with ice to help keep the swelling down. In the middle of tending to my wounds, he started to pray. Being an emergency-room physician, Greg is always very calm. He has seen it all. But the look on his face told me he was concerned. He didn't share this with me then, but his fear was that a blow to the head like that could have caused permanent damage or even been fatal. I had a large flap of skin hanging off my nose and he cleaned my wounds before rushing me to a surgeon to sew me up. Greg explained to me that most people scar from not having their wounds cleaned properly. The dirt has a tattooing effect. If you're not scrubbed carefully, it can cause permanent damage, though this was the least of his worries. I always thought I had a pretty strong threshold for pain, but as we drove to the doctor I was sobbing the entire time.

I started thinking about my speech of a few days earlier about how some people get self-esteem from their appearance, and that nobody can guarantee what you'll look like tomorrow. As I was giving the speech, I remember thinking, Well, maybe that's an exaggeration because the aging process is a gradual process . . . so tomorrow I'm probably going to look pretty much the same. The challenge of my accident reminded me that things can and often do change in an instant. I started thinking, Well, okay, my face has been ripped to shreds, but there are still lots of things I'll be able to do no matter how this turns out.

One thing I didn't know if I'd be able to do was

the sequel to the film *Once upon a Christmas* called *Twice upon a Christmas*. It was a very exciting project in which, once again, I play Santa's daughter. My co-stars were my friends John Dye, from *Touched by an Angel*, a talented, caring man, and Mary Donnelly Haskell, a brilliant artist, wife, and mother. The producers included HRH Prince Edward and my business partners Erik Sterling, Jason Winters, Jon Carrasco, and Stephen Roseberry. In many ways, the film was planned as a reunion of friends and family. Everyone involved shares a loving relationship with the Haskell family: Sam, Mary, Sam IV, and Mary Lane. Sam heads the television division at the William Morris Agency and is one of the entertainment world's most respected men. The doctors made it clear that there was no way I'd be able to start the film on time. I felt both sad and guilty. So many people are involved in the production of a movie. I worried about the unemployment and disappointment my carelessness might cause. At my request, the producers had planned the production schedule to accommodate my children's summer break. I asked if another actor could replace me. Very sweetly, everyone refused. It was a wait-and-see game. When would I heal, and afterward, would I look anything like I used to? We just didn't know. Eventually, the movie was made, and I was able to play the part I had been cast in. It was a huge challenge for the producers to rearrange the schedule yet again, but they were able to work things out so that I could heal properly. I am so grateful for their kindness and understanding.

In the grand scheme of things, I was very blessed. I figured that I'd be laid up in for a few weeks, and hey, that would give me some extra time with my family while I recovered. The truth is, I was extremely fortunate because I could have been killed.

When my face was so completely distorted after this accident, I wasn't really sure how I was going to react. It was a weird feeling for me. But after the pain went away and I stopped hurting and my kids stopped being scared of me, I began to feel such a sense of peace. Things were flashing through my head like, Well, I've had this face for thirty-eight years . . . whatever. I'll have a new face for the next sixty. I began to wonder what my life was going to have in store for me. I started feeling really grateful for the years that I was able to benefit from my appearance, and I have to admit that as superficial as it was, it did help me gain recognition and start a thriving business. I knew that God loves me for who I am and not for what I look like. It's just a face . . . and we all have them. I still had my faith, and that was something that could never be taken away from me.

That accident brought me back to embracing

what I like to call my Plan B life. Plan B has changed
through the years. In my modeling days, it meant if I
walked away and couldn't earn as much money, I'd get
a small apartment, and a nine-to-five job so that I
could get my degree and teach school. Today Plan B
means if my company experiences financial challenges or stops completely, we'd adjust. We'd simplify
our lifestyle even further. The joy of that is that I'd
have even more time with Greg and my most important job, being a mom. It wouldn't change the basic
foundation by which I live my life.

I believe that true self-esteem is attainable to
everyone regardless of background, economic standing, or challenges. I like to think of it as understanding your value. True self-esteem comes from
understanding our value to God. The more we focus
on ourselves, the more insecure and self-absorbed we
become. It's essential to have goals in life, but our self-
value comes from realizing who, how, and with what
we were made. God created us in His own image—so
we can be absolutely certain of our dignity and worth.
You are God's creation, and He is very pleased with
how He made you. His love is unchanging. It's so
important to remember this whenever I am feeling
less valuable or uncertain of my worthiness. Even
with great self-esteem, you will get hurt from time to
time. We are all equally valuable to God. No matter

how difficult your circumstances may be, God will
always be right there along with you, regardless of
what you might be going through. I believe that
we need to use our God-given gifts, which everyone
has (it's just a matter of discovering them), to help
others, which in turn helps us build up our self-
esteem.

True self-esteem esteems others. Loving others as
we love ourselves means actively working to see that
their needs are met while not neglecting our own.
Interestingly, people who focus on others rather than
themselves rarely suffer from low self-esteem. It
reminds me of something I learned from an acting
teacher. He said, "If you want your work in a scene to
be interesting, put the focus on the other person." Or,
as my pastor, Bruce Greene, says, "Don't think less of
yourself, just think of yourself less."

To be powerful, you have to believe you are powerful. Sometimes you will succeed and sometimes you
will fail. If you never fail, you're not risking enough to
live your most fulfilling life. I look at failure as education, and in that respect, I'm very well educated. From
my days as a paper deliverer, I knew that I really liked
being self-employed. Early in my modeling career, I
was looking at different business opportunities that
I could become involved in. Being a lousy cook, I was
very surprised when a friend gave me a book on

making beer to find out that I actually had a talent for this. My first batch was great. I got very carried away with myself. My immediate thought was that this venture would be so profitable. Watch out! I was going to put the big brewers out of business.

The second batch, however, turned out to taste more like a science project. It was very humbling. I spent about two years researching the beer business. I invested my time, energy, money, and resources in this business and became involved in a microbrewery. I ultimately learned that I didn't have a passion for beer. The microbrewery moved forward, but I sold my interest. I didn't give up on business, but I gave up on beer. Success comes from finding and living your passion.

I investigated other businesses, but I didn't have the right partners, and they failed. But these failures have been learning experiences for me. When I wanted to expand and take my Home Collection brand to a different level of distribution, there were people who said, "No, you can't do that. It's never been done. It can't be done." I'm glad that I didn't listen to those people. Last summer, the flooring division of our Home Collection Brand, through my partnership with Shaw Industries, was given the Good Housekeeping Seal, which happens when the Good Housekeeping Institute does a series of tests on products to check out the quality and claims. If everything is to their standards, which are very high, the seal can be awarded. In spite of being told that I couldn't expand my line, I persevered. We need to persevere even when others are unkind. We are honored to partner with Shaw, the world's largest flooring company and a fantastic group of people!

Recently a man told me that he fell in love with me from looking at my picture. But the second I started talking, he said he fell right out of love. I didn't take it as a compliment that he fell in love with my image. The fact that I had opinions and shared them infuriated this guy. He was a shut-up-and-pose kind of person. Words can hurt. They are very powerful. They can build a person up or tear a person down. My self-esteem doesn't depend upon what other people say, think, or do. I accept compliments, and I am grateful if people say nice things. But if they don't, that's okay, too.

Beautiful people come in all shapes, sizes, colors, and ages. God gives us the power to persevere regardless of how others see us, judge us, or treat us. He doesn't make mistakes, and He is always there ready to forgive the ones we make. Sure, we all have our doubts, but it is so important not to tie our inner beauty to anything external. When we're honoring God's word and His will we find our inner strength and learn how truly powerful we are. I find reading scripture powerful. I find caring for my family joyous and empowering. There is great power in working with people who think differently than I do and joy in seeing us all come together to accomplish a common goal. One of the great blessings of traveling all over the world for my various businesses is the unique opportunity to hear what people from every different type of background have to say about their lives. I listen to every word carefully because each of us has different life experiences, and I know we need to learn from each other. Listening to people, especially those with whom you may disagree, helps you discover in your heart and your mind the power God has given to you.

Since I'm painfully shy, I think it's safe to say that God is the only one who knows all of my ugly secrets and thoughts. In spite of that, He still loves me. To have someone love you, and I mean love you completely without condition, is really a remarkable thing. And it's very powerful. Someone once asked me if they could make a movie out of my life, my whole life, every thought, every moment, every detail, how would I feel? My initial reaction was that I would feel mortified. I wouldn't want that. But that's how it is with God. He sees everything, and He stills loves you. I know that God made each of us unique. There

is no one else like you or me. That is great and powerful. God doesn't make mistakes, and His love is
something that is available to everyone. That's the
kind of self-esteem that no one can ever take away.
Remember this and you will always be powerful in the
only way that truly matters.

LESSON TWO

Success in life is achieved by experiencing and
conquering challenges.

- The power of you . . . you are powerful.

- If self-esteem comes from superficial things, we will
  be disappointed.

- True self-esteem is attainable by everyone.

- Failure is an education.

- Find and live your passion.

- Celebrate our differences.

- Don't think less of yourself, think of yourself less.

- Even with great self-esteem you will get hurt from
  time to time.

Chapter Three

POWERFUL FAMILIES

❖ ❖

Inspiration

TRAIN A CHILD IN THE WAY HE
SHOULD GO, AND WHEN HE IS OLD
HE WILL NOT TURN FROM IT.

Proverbs 22:6

I believe there are two kinds of families—the family we are born into and the family we choose. What constitutes a family can be defined in many ways. They range from families like the single mom with several kids living down the block to a multi-generational traditional unit. They are loving, maddening, critical, inspiring, embarrassing, and funny. Dolly Parton once wrote "When you'll forgive someone for what you'd fight others for . . . it's family." Family represents one very important thing: *You are never alone.*

Things my parents taught me stay with me today. My mom always taught me, do unto others as you would have them do unto you. Whenever we'd be in the car and we'd hear a siren, she'd pull over to the side of the road and ask us to pray because the sound meant that somewhere, someone was in trouble. A friend once asked my mother, "How do you know it's not a prank?" Her response shows the essence of my mother's heart—for someone to pull a prank like that means that they're in trouble and they need prayer, too.

There are paths each and every one of us walks as a result of the family we are raised in. Our family is one of the greatest influences on how our lives and the lives of our children will develop. It's essential to establish a strong sense of family togetherness from an early age whenever possible. That starts at home. Home should be a refuge—a place where we renew our faith in family and friends. Practical jokes were a big thing in my home growing up. While celebrating my fifth birthday, my parents presented me with a beautiful cake. I thought that I had successfully blown out all the candles, only to have them continually re-light. As if that wasn't enough, when I opened my first gift, it was a heavy, brick-shaped birthday present, and there was in fact a brick inside the box. I didn't know what to think. Dad couldn't stop laughing, and when he laughs, his whole body shakes, especially his face, but sound doesn't really come out. He finally gave me a real present, a pickup truck that I could sit on and make go by scooting my feet. Dad was always playing practical jokes on us. We usually laughed and joked and appreciated the love that was behind the mischief.

My dad, who was a union labor organizer, was always helping the little guy, the underdog. If people were not being treated fairly, Dad would fight for them. At dinner when Dad would pray, he used to always thank God for making him the richest man in the world. Of course, we had everything we needed, so I took what he was saying quite literally as a child. I believed that we were really rich, as in had a lot of money, which we certainly were not. As I grew older, however, I realized that when my father spoke of prosperity, he in fact wasn't referring to money or material wealth, but to the richness in his life that money cannot buy. He was speaking of his beautiful family and the highest level of love in his life both given and received. My parents had financial difficulties over the years, but I always felt that in every respect that mattered, we were the richest family in the world. I have always tried to carry his perspective with me from the moment I was old enough to understand that difference. Dad and Mom taught us to appreciate the beauty that God created. This spirit that my parents instilled in me as a child has become a common denominator throughout many aspects of my life as an adult.

As a little girl, I remember thinking that my mom was so lucky to have found my dad, and I worried that I would never find anyone who compared to him. I am thankful that I did meet a man who measured up—my husband, Greg. My mom actually played matchmaker. She was working as a nurse in the same hospital where Greg was interning. One day when I was having lunch with her, I saw him walk by. He turned and caught me checking him out. Mom told me what a nice guy he was. After several weeks unsuccessfully trying to bump into him at the hospital again, Mom invited Greg to lunch with us. On that first date, we were both nervous and quiet, but what impressed me was that in spite of the fact that he was in the midst of a one-hundred-hour-plus workweek, he remained gracious and kind. From the time we began dating, people regularly stop me on the street to share with me, not only how well Greg cares for them, but the fact that he takes time for them and demonstrates his concern for them and their families. We dated for two years, married, and now have two incredible children—our son, Erik, who is seven, and our daughter, Lily, who is three.

Being a parent is a full-time job. In fact, I cannot think of anything as difficult, important, or rewarding than being a mother or father. All mothers are working mothers whether you work inside the home or out. When household and/or business duties keep us from our children, we feel guilt. I know I do. Motherhood is a daily challenge of balancing to give our

children the time and attention they deserve and
need and get our many jobs done. Proverbs 31:10–31
is one of my favorite verses in the Bible. It shows a
woman of strong character, great wisdom, great compassion, and many, many skills. She is an excellent
wife and mother. She is also a manufacturer, manager,
importer, realtor, farmer, seamstress, upholsterer, and
merchant. Her strength and dignity do not come from
her amazing achievements, but from her reverence for
God. Her appearance is never mentioned. Her attrac-
tiveness comes entirely from her character. The
woman described has outstanding abilities. In fact,
she may not be one woman at all, but a composite
portrait of womanhood. My days are not long enough
to do all that this woman does, but we can all be
inspired and encouraged by her. Being a stay-at-home
mom can seem a thankless job; however, I cannot
think of a more heroic commitment. Ideally, when
children are young, it would be great if both parents
could stay home in order to spend quality time with
their kids. I also understand that most of us don't have
ideal lives. There are many single parents out there
struggling to support their families and doing a
wonderful job.

In my family, we all still flock to my mom when
there is a family drama going on. It seems like everyone goes to Mom to complain or discuss whatever is

bugging us. She listens and becomes involved without interfering. She tells us to take our issues and confront whomever it is we are having a problem with. My sisters and I are each so different. I love and respect them so much. My older sister, Mary, is extremely loyal, so sweet, gentle, and glamorous. She has the kindest heart. Cynthia is a loving and caring person. Her strength covers her very tender heart. She is an extremely talented actress and comedienne.

I really admire my parents for never showing favoritism in our home. They made each of us feel like their favorite, and they continue to do that today. I took a Bible study class, and it was so interesting to learn about all of the dysfunctional families that are talked about in the text. The jealousy that ensued between Esau and Jacob was a direct result of their parents favoring one over the other.

We have been very careful not to show favoritism with Erik and Lily. My husband and I need the wisdom of Solomon—especially when it comes to sibling squabbles. We avoid comparisons. They are both incredible individuals, and we love them both equally. I explained to Erik when I was pregnant with Lily that our love for him won't have to be shared. Our love for both of our children grows every day. When you are expecting a child, God fills you with a new abundance of love.

I know that I have limited time with our son and daughter and I will never get that time back, so I am going to enjoy every moment that I can—while I can. I think there is so much pressure on women to do it all. I don't believe that people can do it all and have it all at once. Our life comes in seasons and at each season we need to prioritize our time. It's a constant balancing act, but I think that for me, one of the benefits of my work is that I never take my motherhood for granted. I appreciate and savor every day. Mom worked at different times as a stay-home mom, housekeeper, baby sitter, and nurse while she raised three kids, and she continues to be my inspiration.

The foundation of a strong family is striking a balance between realistic and unrealistic expectations. You can be successful with family and work if you plan it right and if you surround yourself with people who share and support your vision.

I am extremely blessed that my mother helps me with my children. I have talked with so many women over the years who say to me how they wish that their mom were still alive or that they wish that they got along better or that she lived in the same state. It is such a blessing that I have my family with me so much of the time. Since both my husband and I have demanding careers, we agreed that we needed to figure out our long-term child-care situation early on. I suggested to Greg that we ask my mom to look after the kids when we couldn't. Greg was concerned at first. He said, "We can fire someone else, but we can't fire your mom if she doesn't work out." And he had a reasonable point, but my mom is so unbelievable— there's no one like her. Greg is the first one to acknowledge that it's worked out beautifully. My mom is one of my heroes, because of her unconditional love.

One of the things that gives me the most joy is being able to focus on just being a mom. After my driveway face plant last year, I was able to spend six weeks at home recuperating. That accident inadvertently gave me the gift of being able to spend more uninterrupted time doing the day-to-day things with my kids that I don't always get to do. It also gave me the chance to catch up with other important people in my life who I don't get to see as often as I would like, such as my grandmother, my sisters, my friends— and especially, my husband. When I am away from home, all I want to do is get back to my family. When you are a busy mom, that's the priority, but sadly, that means when I am home, other people in my life can sometimes feel neglected because all I really want to do is catch up with my kids. I want to take Erik to basketball practice and swim with Lily.

Growing up, everything fun that we did was done together as a family, and I am trying to pass that genuine gift on to our children. We go hiking, biking, fishing, go to the beach and collect seashells and rocks. I hope Erik and Lily will grow up with that same love of family togetherness that my mom and dad gave to my sisters and me.

I have made a decision to put faith and my family first in life. It takes that kind of commitment to make and maintain a powerful family. My husband knows without a doubt that he and our children are more important than my work could ever be, and I know our children and our marriage are his absolute priority. There have been many challenges along the way, too. There's no question that marriage is a lot of work. My mom and dad helped me to understand that it is what you accomplish together as a unit that makes a powerful family. They instilled a belief that in a family you need to build one another up. My husband is an emergency-room physician who often works very long hours. I travel for work more than I would like. If we were in a marriage where we didn't mutually support one another and our busy careers, it could be extremely disconcerting and damaging to our family foundation. We have mutual respect, and our love is something that continues to grow stronger each and every day, especially as we grow and mature as people.

I think that there is a tendency to believe love is an emotion or a feeling rather than a verb or an action. There are days when you might not feel like you love your husband or wife. God commands us to love one another, and it is something that requires work. If it came naturally, it would not be one of God's commandments. It is my love of God and my desire to obey His word that makes it impossible to ever consider not working out my issues with Greg. So many people feel they can simply walk away from a relationship because they no longer feel that love. It's hard work, but it's good work. Putting someone else's needs over your own isn't always easy, believe me, I know. Both my husband and I are pretty headstrong and independent, and we're both control freaks. So, giving over that kind of control is challenging for us, but starting each day out by asking what can I do for my husband today sure beats walking around the house asking, what have you done for me lately? We try to talk and communicate our feelings if something is bothering us, but now that we have two children, it's a little harder to finish those conversations than it used to be. We always talk about important issues, such as our ideas on parenting and our children's lives, and there are definitely things that we don't agree on, including some political issues. But when it comes to raising our children, we agreed from the beginning that we were going to be a team and that we would not undermine the other person. What we learn as children greatly influences who we become as adults. I remind myself of that today as a parent and carefully monitor the lessons and values I give to my kids.

You have to be consistent in front of your children, because they are so smart—they catch everything. Our kids are really sharp, and we can't put on an act for them. We have to live our words and actions, or else they'll see right through us. Having children has made us a stronger couple and made us work harder on getting along. We can't be as childish and dramatic as we used to be before becoming parents. There's really no benefit in trying to drag a fight out (even if I was right . . .), and that knowledge has forced us to resolve our issues in a much quicker manner and to be more forgiving and understanding of each other and our needs. The kids really force us to work through our problems and communicate because we want to set a good example for them, and we're trying to instill a solid family foundation for their future. It's a big responsibility preparing your children for the world.

In times of celebration and in times of trouble, we

have a tendency to reach out and connect with our loved ones and put our petty bickering aside. Family, whether homemade or chosen, can provide enduring strength and unparalleled love and support. They say that blood is thicker than water, but I am not sure that I agree with that sentiment. These days, especially since the events of September 11, I find myself reevaluating the meaning, importance, and impact of family. I find myself remembering people of every race, religion, income level, and political ideology who put all of their differences aside to stand together as one united family—to band together and rise above the rhetoric to hold hands, pray together, and do whatever it took to help the families of the victims cope with the loss of their loved ones.

Though we cannot choose the family we are born into, we certainly can develop relationships with friends that become our family of choice. Last summer, I was faced with a personal challenge when my father became ill and I was getting ready to head to Vancouver to shoot the Christmas movie. With my father's health concerns, my mom needed to be with my dad. She wasn't able to join me on the set to help take care of my kids as she usually does. Dad's health crisis stabilized, but he wasn't entirely out of the woods. My husband couldn't leave his job for any extended period of time either. There

are very few people in the world whom I feel comfortable enough with to care for Erik and Lily, but my
dear friend and business partner Jon Carrasco is on
that very short list. Jon is one of five partners in
Sterling-Winters Company, the marketing and management firm which is partnered with Kathy Ireland
WorldWide. Had it not been for Jon, and our family
friend, Maria Rodriguez, our children would most certainly have wanted to go home, leaving me behind to
fulfill my obligations to the movie. Maria has such a
caring heart, that you instantly feel her love, our children always do. The show would have gone on, but
my heart would have been broken at not having Erik
and Lily with me. Uncle Jon's love of life and sense of
adventure and fun has been a gift to them and has
made an impact on my whole family in ways he may
never know. Jon is an incredibly busy man, who took
care of his daily business issues, worked on the film
deal, uprooted his own life to be with us in Vancouver, and cared for my children as if they were his own.
His devotion blew me away then and continues to
overwhelm me each and every day. Jon gave me an
essential sense of peace while I had to work. Not only
did I not have to worry, I was secure knowing that
they were all having fun together, which allowed
me to focus on my performance without a care in
the world.

All of my partners in Sterling-Winters are part
of my extended family. I don't imagine that Erik
Sterling, Jason Winters, Jon Carrasco, and Stephen
Roseberry will ever fully know how much each of
them means to me and my immediate family. I'm not
always great at expressing my feelings, partly because
words can't adequately describe the respect, gratitude,
and love I have for each of them. If they could look
inside my heart, they would see it written there.

Creating a family of choice is the opportunity to
surround yourself with people who enhance your life.
It doesn't always mean that those relationships are
any easier than the ones we have with our biological
family. Indeed, family, in every sense of the word, is
about challenging ourselves to become better people
and empower one another. We learn our deepest
truths through our relationships.

I don't make friends very easily. I am cautious
about letting too many people into my life. I learned
to value good friends at a young age, because there
was a time when I didn't have any. When I made a
friend, it was like finding a buried treasure. It is such
a special thing. I never want to take it for granted.
When people do come into my life, I cherish them.
My friends are certainly a diverse group of people,
which I really appreciate. I think there can be value
in creating a family of choice where you don't choose

people who are just like the family you were born into
or the friends you're comfortable with. Otherwise it
could be very boring if everyone shared the same
opinions and points of view. Who wants to have
friends just like themselves? Don't be afraid of differences. Be sure to have people in your life who support
your core values, so that you are able to stand up to
peer pressure, but it's interesting to have friends with
different opinions and points of view. This causes me
to think and grow.

For many years I justified not going to church regularly because I was so busy, and I believed strong
enough not to need a church family. I felt since God
is everywhere, I could be close to Him wherever I
happened to be. Once again I was humbled. I found
out that I wasn't as strong as I thought I was. I learned
that depending on others for encouragement and support is not a sign of weakness but wisdom and
strength. I get a great sense of belonging to the
strongest kind of family when I am close to my church
and its congregants. I am so grateful to Pastor Bruce,
his wife, Marilu, and my church family for their love,
support, and encouragement over the years. I'm also
so grateful to the women in my weekly Bible study
and to Jeannine Morgan and all the moms and dads
who participate in the parenting classes for their wisdom, compassion, and love. My closest friends on

earth are my husband, children, parents, sisters, and
my best friends, Camille, Jenny, and Baret, whom I
have known since we were teenagers. They are always
there for me in good times and in bad and they are
truly family. From my dear sweet friend, Florence,
who is ninety-eight years old, to Erik, Jason, Jon, and
Stephen—each as different as can be. If you lined up
my friends in a room, you'd probably be surprised that
we were all friends because we're all so different yet
each have similar qualities. We try not to get too
caught up in superficial things, and all of us follow our
hearts.

The family we create is extremely powerful. In
business, it is critical that we have a one-on-one relationship with people. I get to work with a team of
geniuses every day. I am so blessed to say that I love
the people I work with, and they are family. It didn't
start out that way. We started out as strangers, and it
took years to build trust, but as time went on and trust
was built we learned about each other's work ethic,
commitment, and core values. We don't agree on
everything. Absolutely not! We agree to disagree in
an agreeable way, but we share the same core values.
And all of those qualities are so important. I came to
these people twelve years ago for guidance and repre-
sentation. Today, it amazes me that together we've
built Kathy Ireland WorldWide.

Everybody is unique and different. The things that I value most in people are integrity, sincerity, loyalty, honesty, and the knowledge that I can trust them. Most people want their friends to have those qualities. Few can say that they do. I love that each of my friends is a wonderful person who brings a tremendous amount of love and joy to my life. My business partners are excellent examples of surrounding myself with people who enhance and empower my life.

You already know I wanted to quit the modeling business. I was constantly trying to figure out what I was going to do next. Business was always something that appealed to me.

It became clear that I was going to need to find managers to help get my vision off the ground and start expanding my career. I had already been represented by a management company that wasn't fulfilling my vision for the future. When it came time to make a move, I really wanted to find the right partners—partners who shared my same views and had the ability to think outside the box. I was concerned about making the right decision because a manager can work for or against you—especially in my business. I even questioned whether I truly needed a manager at all. Being as independent as I am, my idea of a manager was somebody who would get all involved in my life and try to tell me what to do. I thought, Who needs that?

In spite of my hesitations, I decided to have a meeting with Erik Sterling and Jason Winters, one of three references I had been given. The way Jason tells the story is that he didn't want to meet me. He had absolutely no interest, and he had his doubts about my abilities. Jon Carrasco, now a partner at Sterling-Winters Company and then Jason's assistant, was adamant about Jason meeting me. He threatened to quit the company if Jason chose not to. Jon's attitude was a testament of how powerful a person can be. He confronted the CEO of the company and suddenly my meeting was on Jason's agenda. Jon is now the Creative Director and Executive Vice President of Kathy Ireland WorldWide.

I went to their offices, which were special. Yes, they were beautiful, but more important, there was a tremendous sense of energy and family that I noticed immediately. There were a lot of people working there, which was very different from my last team of managers. I didn't know what to think. I wanted to understand exactly what all of these people did around the office. I wanted to know everything about how they ran their company. I was looking for partners who would last.

I explained to Jason that I was a hard worker and

wasn't afraid to do whatever I needed to expand my career. I also explained that I had boundaries that weren't flexible. I live in Santa Barbara, and it was very important to me to maintain a separate professional and personal life. I spoke of my faith and expressed how critical it was to me to honor my beliefs. I wouldn't sacrifice my family time to attend Hollywood parties with people I didn't know, which is common for someone trying to break through in the entertainment business. I spoke of my husband and the family we would someday have. I clearly voiced that I wouldn't compromise any of those priorities for work. Those were my boundaries and that's how I wanted to work. I was certain that Jason was going to kick me out of his office for being a pain. But he didn't.

It was ironic that at twenty-seven years old I was already feeling like an aging model. With my passion for business and my background in fashion, I felt a career in design might be possible if I partnered with the right people. I wasn't sure exactly what I wanted to do when I left his office that day. I was thoughtful. Jason said he'd love to work with me. I told him that I would have to let him know. The thing that really struck me during our meeting was that Jason is a very good listener. That is so important. He listened to everything I said, and that was something I hadn't always experienced in business. As a model, I had been dismissed so many times. People would twist my words. I wanted to be in business with someone I could rely on to listen to what I was saying and represent my ideas exactly as I shared them—not as they wanted to convey them.

I weighed my decision very carefully. I needed to feel completely comfortable about everything. All my instincts told me that Sterling-Winters Company was the way to go. It's kind of funny because Jason has told me that after all these years he feels like I'm his manager. I find that so humorous considering that we almost never met.

There was never a hidden agenda when I began working with my new team. They aren't motivated by money or greed, but by truth and trust, and they cared for my well-being from day one. I just felt that their motives were pure—so pure that I felt kind of embarrassed when I first started working with them. They represented many famous people who were surely making a lot more money for them than I was, but they always treated me the same as any other client. I would be embarrassed when they would attend a meeting with me. I just could never fathom how they could justify taking time from their own busy schedules to help shape and guide my career—and my future. Today when we attend meetings, people may think I have an entourage. The truth is, I am there with my partners and people on our team who all have critical jobs to do.

It takes me a long time to extend my trust to people. I don't naturally do it, but over time as relationships grow and strengthen, trust is one of the most important aspects between people. I have definitely learned that it takes years to build trust and respect, but only a moment to destroy it. Jason Winters is one of those people in my life who has a way of making people believe in themselves. He believed in me from the day we met and showed me that I could do anything, even the things I knew I was terrible at. At a time when others were just about to put me out to pasture, Jason listened to me and had an incredible ability to visualize a future with amazing insight and external light. Although we have had our differences, he has never judged me and I have never judged him. We both choose to celebrate our differences and that has allowed us to grow in so many ways as people, partners, friends, and family. Jason uses every gift God has given him. He is blessed with vision, great thoughtfulness, wisdom, compassion, endurance, and love. Jason is a rare and special person. Those who know him understand exactly what I mean. He gives of himself to others tirelessly around the clock. The experience I get from working with

Jason is so fulfilling and our process together is unlike anything I have ever known. Having Jason in my life is a powerful blessing. Jason has taught me to open my eyes and heart to look at people and situations a little differently—and a lot better, because he showed me how to have more love and compassion for others. Through my relationship with Jason I have learned more patience, forgiveness, and love in all of my relationships. He showed me how to turn hurt and anger into love, a gift I will always treasure.

From a career standpoint, there was so much opportunity out there to explore and use, which we have done together as a team. I still don't believe I've reached my full potential. There's a lot more work to do. We have our differences in terms of approach, but we're always up front with each other about who we are. When it came down to core issues such as integrity and tenacity, we were always on the same page. No one pretended to be something we were not. Over time we built a level of trust that gave all of us a level of comfort to not fear reaching our highest potential. It is so important to find and surround yourself with the right people—people who share your vision and have the ability to tap into that potential inside each of us to become the best we can be.

I never had a family business, but today I have a business family. I try to treat everyone I work with the same way I would treat my own family. Having a family, whether by marriage or merger has given me the greatest sense of security and support in business and in life.

LESSON THREE

A strong family foundation will influence you and your loved ones for life.

- Things you learn as a child and teach as a parent last a lifetime.
- It takes years to build trust and respect, but a moment to destroy it.
- We learn our deepest truths through our relationships.
- There are two kinds of families—the family we are born into and the family we choose.
- With family you are never alone.

Chapter Four

POWERFUL ANSWERS

❖ ❖

Inspiration
ASK AND IT WILL BE GIVEN TO YOU;
SEEK AND YOU WILL FIND.
Matthew 7:7–8

Every day I realize how much more there is that I need to know. The more I learn, the more I realize that my life must be a work in progress. My website, kathyireland.com, was developed specifically for the purpose of sharing information with people, especially busy moms. Initially we felt the website would be a wonderful way to connect with people and provide solutions. We weren't prepared for how much *we* would learn. Every day we hear from women telling us what they like and what they don't like. As an entrepreneur, my need for information is critical in taking action and providing responses. My website provides invaluable feedback, which is vital to understanding our customers' needs and making whatever changes necessary to help fulfill them. The more I listen to everything being said about our products and services, the faster I can respond with determination to make them work. That approach isn't limited to my role as a designer. It serves me in every area of life.

It is imperative to understand the importance of asking powerful questions. The art of eliciting powerful answers is knowing what questions to ask. The right questions open doors to essential information. When someone tells me no, I always ask why?, and if they say yes, I ask how? These are my two favorite questions. Develop your own favorite questions and don't be afraid to overcome your fears to ask and seek information. One of my early challenges was pretending through silence to understand things that weren't clear. My parents always taught me there are no foolish questions. Why did it take so many years for me to appreciate that wisdom?

Communication is important in every relationship. Whether you realize it or not, you are always communicating. Is the communication clear? Is it powerful? Does it serve the needs of the people involved? Parents must communicate with their children. Husbands and wives must communicate. Partners, friends, business associates, family members, customers, teachers are people we communicate with. Good communication is a learned skill. I know that for years it was a strong challenge for me. For a long time, just as I didn't choose to see the world clearly, I didn't ask certain questions because I was afraid of the

answers. Here's how I've learned to communicate. I
listen and try to process what is being said, think
about my response, and hopefully then communicate
my feelings. I'm not a great spontaneous communica-
tor. My friends, family, and business associates have
accused me of overthinking everything. I accept that
happily. It works for me. I think most people want and
need to be listened to. Becoming a good listener has
helped me develop my relationships with healthy,
strong bonds.

When I first met my husband, he and I had different points of view about marriage. He viewed
marriage as just a piece of paper. I didn't see it that
way. Greg and I dated for a year and a half before he
proposed. I was taken by surprise when he finally did.
Talk about important questions and answers!

I have to confess that I thought he was going to
ask me sooner. The Christmas before Greg proposed,
I had dropped in at his house while he was at work.
He had a little Christmas tree with presents all
around. There were two in particular that caught my
eye—the ones that read Kathy. One box was larger
and the other was perfectly small . . . like a ring box.
I had asked for a Walkman, which I figured might be
the bigger box.

My curiosity was getting the best of me. I called
some of my girlfriends and asked if they thought I

should snoop? Granted, it's not the most ethical thing, but let's face it . . . I was a woman in love— what were my choices? I'm sure that all guys know women snoop—if they don't they do now!

I snuck a peek at the larger box and, sure enough, it was my Walkman. My friends tried to convince me to open the smaller box. They were certain it was a ring. I just kept saying no. I didn't want to spoil it if it turned out that it was an engagement ring. I wanted to be surprised. As hard as it was, I am so proud I did not open that box.

I went home and told my mom, sisters, and best friends what I had done. Everyone made me promise to call first thing Christmas morning to share the good news. Christmas day arrived, and I went to Greg's house in the most festive mood. I sat on the floor slowly opening the larger box first and feigned my surprise. "Oh, thank you, Greg!" He then handed me the little box. My heart was pounding. I couldn't believe this moment had arrived. I slowly pulled the wrapping off the box and looked down at my beautiful new set of batteries! Yup. He gave me batteries! I was definitely surprised! The moral of this story is simple: Sometimes we don't always get the answers we're looking for, but we always get answers. We may not like the answer. We may not agree with the answer. But the answer always comes . . . this time mine came in the form of double As. I eventually confessed to Greg what I had done. He thought it was pretty funny, and he told me he would have proposed sooner but he was saving up to buy me the ring he really wanted to get for me.

Greg finally did propose to me three months later on my twenty-fifth birthday. My good friend Camille hosted a birthday party for me. She invited all of my friends and family. Greg's parents, Phil and Barbara, were there and gave me beautiful pearl earrings. They were exceptionally warm that night—I didn't have a clue about what was going to happen.

The next night, Greg had his own idea about how to celebrate my birthday. He was living in his cottage bachelor pad at the time. It was one tiny all-purpose room that served as his kitchen, bathroom, bedroom, and living room, and he didn't have much furniture. His dining table was actually a picnic table. Greg is a wonderful cook, so he decided to make me dinner. It was funny, because when I showed up he was wearing a tie, and Greg is very casual. After dinner, Greg brought out dessert—a birthday cake with a single candle on top. As I blew out the candle I noticed the ring around the candle. I was so happy— and immediately accepted his proposal.

God gave us two ears and one mouth for a reason. One of my favorite quotes from the Bible is "be quick to listen, slow to speak, and slow to anger." (James 1:19–20) It makes the important point that one's faith and actions are expressed by what they do. I sometimes find myself challenged by that quote. I am prone to stew about something instead of confronting the issue. I continually have to work it through and pray to follow that quote.

About nine years ago, I was driving to Los Angeles for an audition. I had recently made a decision that, moving forward, I would try my hardest to be aware of how my choices were affecting others. As far as acting was concerned, I decided I would not take on any role that glorified behavior that I felt would be displeasing to God. (Because I remained such a baby Christian for quite a long time, some of the choices I made then, I would not make today. I hope as time goes on I will mature in my faith and that my choices will reflect God's will more and more.) The audition was for a movie of the week. The topic was abortion. The project claimed that it was simply showing both sides of the issue, but it clearly had a pro-choice slant. This presented no problems for me because even though I became Christian at age eighteen, I was pro-choice. (I have since found several passages in the Bible that make it clear how God feels about abortion. Somehow I missed those verses.) As a woman who always has and always will fight for women's rights it made sense. While I didn't know if I could ever go through such a procedure, who was I to tell another woman what she could or could not do with her body?

Traffic was slow, so I had plenty of time to think about this issue. Probably more time than I ever had given in the past. By the time I got to the audition there was a room full of actors waiting to be seen. I had even more time and the more I thought the more I realized I had a lot of questions regarding the issue. Questions that I had never even pondered before. When it was my turn to go in, the producers were very friendly. They said this was an important movie for women. In a kind tone one of the producers said to me, "You are pro-choice aren't you?" I looked at him and said, "Yes." But at that moment I realized I wasn't pro-choice. For me, I knew I was in the worst place imaginable. I was on the fence. I hate being wishy-washy, especially on matters of significance, but with these newfound questions unanswered, I didn't know where I stood. I completely choked at the audition. That was the end of that project but it was only the beginning of my growing questions and my quest for answers.

Upon arriving home that evening, I immediately pulled out the medical textbooks from the book-shelves. From Greg's medical-school days we have an abundance of such books in our home. These are un-biased, purely scientific books which contain no moral perspective. I figured this would be the best place to get my questions answered. I just wanted the facts, not the emotion that gets tied to this issue. My first question was, "What is it?" We first have to know what it is before we can decide if it is okay to kill it. As I read, I learned that from the moment of concep-tion a new life comes into being. At the moment of conception this new life has a complete genetic blueprint. The sex is determined, the blood type is determined, and this new life continues to grow and change until it dies. So I knew it was a life, but what kind of life was it? According to the Law of Biogene-sis, all life comes from preexisting life and each species reproduces after its own kind. Human beings can only reproduce human beings. From there I got my hands on every book I could find on the topic, including *Precious Unborn Human Persons* by Gregory Koukl and *Real Choices* by Frederica Matthews-Green. I asked my pro-choice friends for all the literature they could get for me supporting the right to choose abortion. I was stunned that after learning that the unborn was indeed a human being, the arguments in favor of terminating this life felt so weak. One of the big arguments for choice was that this was not a human being but a potential human being. It's just a mass of cells and if you get it early enough it doesn't even look like a baby. As Mr. Koukl points out in his book, the unborn does not look like a baby the same way a baby does not look like a teenager. But that unborn human being looks exactly the way human beings are supposed to look at that stage of development. We're just not used to seeing humans at their earliest stages, but technology has come a long way since Roe vs. Wade.

It became clear to me that while an unplanned pregnancy causes many complex social issues for women that *must* be addressed, abortion is not a women's rights issue, but a human rights issue. The baby the woman is carrying in her body is not a part of her. This unborn person has a unique fingerprint. There is a very good chance that the baby this woman is carrying can have a different blood type than she has. This unborn person can be male. Since the woman certainly does not have a penis, the unborn is clearly not a part of her body, he simply resides there. I do believe that if a mother's life is in jeopardy, abortion is an appropriate option. In that situation you are not acting to kill but to save. It is unfortunate that the unborn person dies in the process, but you are acting to save a life, the life of the mother. Many arguments in favor of abortion are strong arguments for birth control but not for terminating the life of someone who has already come into existence. Most of the arguments for abortion involve impacts of the social issues concerning a crisis pregnancy. These are important issues that must be addressed. I believe that anyone who takes the life position has the responsibility not only to do everything in their power to make sure that these unborn human beings have the right to be born, but to make sure that once they are born their needs are met. We also need to do all that we can for women who find themselves in a crisis-pregnancy situation. I believe the unborn are not the only victims of abortion but the mothers and fathers are hurt by this as well. I believe this is the most unliberating thing that can be done to a woman and the most emasculating thing that can be done to a man. It goes against our basic nature of protecting our young.

Women have been told by society that this is a quick and simple procedure. When a woman goes to a clinic she is often times not told what her unborn baby looks like. Most often she is not told of the abilities of her unborn at this stage of life. Most often she is not told that what she is about to abort is a human being. How can she make an intelligent choice when she is not given all the facts? While no one really wants to have an abortion, society has told us it is our

God-given right. We are made to feel antiwoman for opposing it. As a woman and a mother of a daughter, I believe nothing could be farther from the truth. While abortion may sound liberating, the decision is often impacted by tremendous external pressures. But it is the woman who must live with the emotional, spiritual, and physical consequences of her decision. God forgives abortion. Nothing is too big for God but oftentimes it is difficult for us to accept that forgiveness. A close friend of Greg's, Dale Dellar, made a profound comment during one of our discussions. We know that by the grace of God, all children have salvation. They are not yet accountable and the unborn babies will go directly to heaven. There is a very good chance that the mother who has aborted her baby will also have salvation. But if we, as Christians, condemn that woman for her pro-choice beliefs or actions, we can jeopardize her salvation. She will most likely feel that she wants nothing to do with this Christian person who attacked her and nothing to do with God if that's what people who follow God are like. Not only could she turn away from God, but she'll tell ten of her friends what jerks Christians are. When we are faced with a difficult situation, we need to ask ourselves a question, "What would Jesus do?" He always responded to people with love. Life is really hard and often messy. We need to not waste our time judging others, but roll up our sleeves and do whatever we can for people who are in an unwanted-pregnancy situation.

Growing up in the seventies I was convinced that equality between men and women meant that we had to be the same. I now understand that God made both man and woman in His image. Our differences are God-given and meant to be celebrated not to oppress one another. No matter how hard a man tries, he will never be able to give birth. This does not make him less valuable as a human being; we are just different. God has chosen to give women the tremendous honor and responsibility of bearing children. I don't like labels. They cause us to dismiss one another assuming we know all there is to know about the person. I am saddened that abortion has become a political issue. Until all sides are willing to work together I fear this atrocity will continue. I am conservative on some issues and liberal on some issues. When it comes to protecting the human rights of the unborn, I am extremely liberal. The bottom line is this, if the unborn is not a human being, women ought to be able to have as many abortions as they want, whenever they want. It doesn't matter. No justification is necessary. If, on the other hand, the unborn is a human being, no justification is adequate unless another human life, the mother's, is at risk.

My beliefs are very unpopular with many people. I have asked leading researchers and doctors to please show me some evidence that the unborn is not a human being. No one has been able to do this. The scientific evidence I see clearly demonstrates the unborn is indeed a human being. Until someone can prove otherwise, I will continue to fight for the human rights of the unborn and to do whatever I can for people who are affected by unwanted pregnancies. I didn't want to be pro-life, but when you ask powerful questions, you get powerful answers. We need to be ready for them.

Learning to forgive and getting out of a judgmental way of thinking helps me to keep close to that slow to speak, slow to anger behavior. If it's something that is too difficult to let go of, I try to open my heart to forgiveness. Forgiveness means that I don't place myself in judgment. While I am able to forgive, it doesn't leave any room for someone who abuses me. With free will, I will choose to engage with someone or not, depending upon the quality of the relationship.

I used to work with a woman who regularly became verbally abusive toward me. After a particularly bad conversation, I decided to ask her to resign from my team. She did, and I never heard from her again until she needed something from me. I had to take a step back and ask myself where she was coming from. I wondered if she was angry with me like I had been with her? Was she having a hard time forgiving me like I had with her? My husband says that I am a person with very high expectations of others. I am a pretty rational thinker, and I hope for others around me to be rational. But, most of us aren't rational all the time. People handle circumstances in many different ways. It was hard for me to reassess that situation—to take a step back and ask myself those questions about this former team member. I realized her abusive behavior stemmed from unresolved pain in her life. Finally I was able to let it go. I try to be consistent in my efforts to avoid anger, bitterness, or even greed. I want to settle differences so that we can come together instead of drift apart. Through forgiveness, I have learned to never allow myself to be in destructive situations. When I find myself there, I don't allow it to keep happening.

Since life is a journey, I want to feel like I am making the best choices along the way. I try to follow Jesus by asking, what would Jesus do in any particular situation. How would He treat this person? That's something that I continually work on. Who am I to judge or criticize another person that God has made in His image? I'll sit down with someone and try to listen to their perspective so that we can resolve any conflict or challenge. Although I try not to harbor ill will, I do have a very long memory.

Sometimes, I find myself inappropriately taking on someone else's struggles. In these cases, they would almost always be better served by my helping them through their challenging times instead of making their challenges my own. This happens a lot in families. If a member of my family is having personal challenges, it's hard for me not to become more involved than I should be. It's that line between support and smothering that we all must be conscious of. I work to keep an open mind and an open heart and try to remain nonjudgmental and avoid making their problems mine. When someone I love is feeling pain I encourage them to pray for guidance and seek powerful answers, as I pray for them as well. Recently, someone I love was facing a true crisis. A series of circumstances caused everything he held dear to be in jeopardy. During this time of pain and difficulty the only possible powerful answer for this situation was a miracle. One was given. During this dilemma, he prayed. Jesus came into his heart. He became a Christian, and the Lord has lifted him up during a time that would otherwise be impossible or bleak. He asked a

wonderful question and received the most powerful
answer.

Having God at the center of our lives, our families, and our relationships gives us a feeling of comfort
and peace through the good and bad times we all
experience. If we trust in Him, He will guide us
through all of our decisions. Through God, I have
been able to make better choices in my life, and that
is the core and foundation of everything I am part of.
I choose good people to be in my life. I try to mediate
conflict rather than ignoring it. I have a tendency to
try to handle certain issues on my own, but when I
include God in my decision process and follow His
lead, I am given a sense of security that I am on the
right path.

Someone once told me that a heart filled with
anger has no room for love. I try to take my ego out of
my questions and answers. I'll refer back to the Bible
because to me it is the best source of information. It
talks about ways to handle every circumstance. I can
look up any situation—acceptance, marriage, anger,
greed, grief, children, sibling rivalry, gratitude, leader-
ship, love, mistakes, money, taxes—the Bible speaks
of it all. I sometimes become reacquainted with a
familiar quote that fits whatever situation I am in
the middle of, and other times I learn something
new about handling an old issue. I know I've shared

this with you earlier, but it is so important to remember that the Bible is the best place to seek divine inspiration and the most powerful answers.

Part of my personal journey is to find the strength and courage to make difficult decisions. We held the first Kathy Ireland LPGA Invitational golf tournament in 2000, which was the fruition of an idea that our team developed five years earlier. The legendary Dinah Shore was one of the first women to host an LPGA event, and what an honor it was to be following in her footsteps. I was very excited because the event was also a fundraiser for a nonprofit organization. Scheduled to play in our Program was an incredible young man, Justin DeLong, who was fourteen years old at the time and very ill from leukemia. It was Justin's dream to compete in a professional golf tournament. It was a bittersweet situation seeing this extraordinary young man compete and win, while demonstrating such courage, because shortly thereafter he lost his life. Justin's spirit will always be inspiring to me.

The tournament was located in South Carolina and at the time the state was immersed in a major controversy over the flying of the Confederate flag that made things awkward. I am often confronted with controversy, but I try not to let the fear of confrontation make me run away. This was a particularly

uncomfortable circumstance because there was pressure from the NAACP to boycott the tournament
unless the flag was removed from the state capitol. As
the tournament date approached, we were assured the
issues surrounding the flag would be resolved. We
found that wasn't the case. I support the philosophies
of the NAACP and my take on this particular circumstance was that if the flag was a cause of discom-
fort because it symbolized pain and suffering, then it
was worth taking a second look at the issue. I really
agonized over what to do about the tournament and
the level of my involvement. In order for me to make
a proper decision, one that felt most comfortable to
me, I needed to seek out all of the information, from
all sides. I couldn't go with or against the boycott just
because other people thought that I should. I make
my own decisions based on my own beliefs. We had
worked so hard to get the tournament off the ground
and here it was, the home stretch, and I wanted to
make sure that no one, especially on my team, was
spinning the situation to make it happen the way they
wanted it to.

As you know, I love and respect the people I work
with and we don't always agree. This was one of those
times. Against their advice, I called the head of the
NAACP to discuss their perspective, and I carefully
weighed what they had to say. I didn't want them to

think that I was in any way undermining their position by hosting the tournament. I wanted to explore
the options and possible solutions so that the families
and especially the children benefiting from the money
raised from the tournament would not lose out. I
thought that there might even be a way that I could
help the NAACP through the press as I was promoting the event. I explained that the effort was for a
nonprofit organization and at the late hour it would
be impossible to move the tournament to another
location. My pulling out of the tournament meant
that many of the sponsors would also pull out their
support, and their generous financial contributions
would be lost. While I understood their position, I felt
strongly that this was not a commercial event and
that it wouldn't be right for me to boycott it even
though I understood the NAACP's position on the
flag issue. I was able to work with the NAACP to
relay to the media that though the tournament would
go on as planned, there would be no way to bring
the event back to the state next year under the same
circumstances. And I didn't.

Though the LPGA golf tournament in South
Carolina was, in itself, a very big success, making the
decision to stand by my commitment had its consequences. I was judged by many. Some said I attacked
their flag, which was not true. South Carolina is a

beautiful state, and I met so many wonderful people there. There are so many beautiful gracious traditions in the southern part of our country. I look forward to bringing an event for my company back to that state in the future.

During a press conference in Myrtle Beach, a reporter asked if I'd be willing to return to the state while the flag controversy was still raging. I said it would be inappropriate for me, being an outsider, to comment on the policy of their state, however, I said that I believed that if there's any symbol that causes people pain, it must be examined for everyone's sake. Some people didn't appreciate this answer. I got hugs from some people and stare-downs from others. At the tournament, a sponsor approached me and shook my hand. As he held my hand, he stared me straight in the eye and said, "I'm so glad we got this flag issue resolved. And it is resolved." What he implied was, "Look little girl, don't mess with something you know nothing about." He was clearly a man who didn't care for my answer. It was hard for me to receive such hostility, but I managed. Giving and receiving powerful answers makes you stronger.

I often find that powerful answers come from very unexpected places. In the end, following our conversation, the NAACP decided not to boycott the tournament. Their willingness to hear my questions and open their hearts to give a powerful answer was a wonderful blessing and experience, for which I will always be grateful.

When I initially launched my home furniture collection, I was extremely concerned that the partner we chose to go into business with share the same kind of philosophy as I did about everything from the quality of their products to the working conditions in the factories. We found a wonderful company with good people, who shared our values and who made an incredible product. We became friends. Yet, with everything we had in common, we had a hard time serving our customers because of pricing and distribution issues. It reminded me of my rock-selling days. The furniture was very beautiful, but not accessible to my primary customer. I became concerned and began questioning how we could address the various challenges we were facing. Eventually we realized that although we cared for each other deeply, we were a better fit as friends than business partners. We began working with Standard Furniture, one of the largest companies in America today. We also share values and now are able to meet my customers' needs. Asking my first partners why we were challenged led us all to the answer that we weren't meant to work together. Today three companies, the first partner, my new partner, and my own company, have all benefited from the tough questions and the real answers.

I HAVE NO GREATER JOY THAN THIS;
TO HEAR MY CHILDREN WALKING IN
THE TRUTH.

3 John 4

Some of the best questions I hear come from my children. I think their questions provoke a need in me to want to seek the truth so that when I answer, I can answer with confidence and security that I am guiding them correctly. If you teach children how to lie, they will remember it all their lives. Do you have trouble with being honest? Many of us do. Can you look back at your life and determine where that pattern began? Anne Frank once wrote, "I believe most people are good." I know that's true. Some of the most dishonest people aren't able to see themselves clearly. Deception is something frequently learned in our childhood. Greg and I are working very hard to help our children understand that there is no place for dishonesty in healthy living. One of the greatest challenges we face as parents is striking a balance between diplomacy and honesty.

One day I was talking to my son, Erik, about heaven. A friend of ours had a dog that died, and he wanted to know if dogs go to heaven like people do. I called an old pastor of mine who has since moved from Santa Barbara and asked him if he believed that dogs go to heaven. He said that he didn't think they did. I asked him where it said that animals don't go to heaven in the Bible. We were on the phone for a long time looking up passages, and we came to the conclusion that animals most likely do go to heaven. The Bible talks about the lion lying down with the lamb, and the child playing with the snake and it describes these different animal beasts and, to me, it seems they would be in heaven together in the most perfect way imaginable.

The book of Revelation says "He will wipe every tear from their eyes. There will be no more death or mourning or crying or pain, for the old order of things has passed away" (Revelation 21:4). Throughout the Bible, Jesus talks about preparing the perfect place for each of us, and since He knows each of us, we can be assured that what He is preparing is perfect. Heaven is a place where there is no more sickness, tears, death, or destruction. I don't think that we're supposed to understand all things about heaven here on earth, but I'm joyous that we were able to answer my son's question.

LESSON FOUR

*Powerful answers come from meaningful and
important questions.*

- When someone tells you no, ask why. When someone tells you yes, ask how.

- Overcome your fears to ask questions and seek information.

- You must ask for what you need.

- Be a good listener.

- Be quick to listen; slow to speak; and slow to become angry.

- Some of the best questions I hear come from children—their innocence illuminates.

- When you ask powerful questions, you get powerful answers. We need to be ready for them.

Chapter Five

POWERFUL CHANGES

❖ ◈

Inspiration
FOR I HAVE LEARNED TO BE CONTENT
WHATEVER THE CIRCUMSTANCES
Phil 4:11

In life, the only thing that is certain is change.
Change is a given. Change is expanding and con-
tracting. We must learn to meet, embrace, and dance
with change. It is something we're always going to
face. Change is constant motion. We can have a neat
life all planned out, but God has a master plan that
may not coincide with our plans. Learning to plan for
change is a lot like planning for a vacation. You know
it's coming—why not be prepared? Growth is preparing for change. We sometimes fear change because we
assume it's negative. Graduation is a change. Marriage
is a change. A new promotion is a change. Achieving
a goal you've set is a change. Those are all great
accomplishments. Be sure you take the time to celebrate them.

I have experienced many changes in my life. If
God grants me a long life, I anticipate so many more.
Up until now, the greatest change in my life was

becoming a mother. Having children is definitely a life-altering change—the most wonderful in every sense of the word. Our children bring tremendous joy to our lives. There are certain ways you live your life before you decide to have kids. Once they arrive, nothing is ever the same. My ability and desire to travel for work shifted after the children were born. My marriage is very different as well. Becoming parents encouraged Greg and me to make some real adjustments. We both had to become less selfish. We each had to become more responsible. We had to be more careful than ever. We learned quickly that children absorb everything, and they pay much more attention to how you live and behave than what you say. We insist on a safe, healthy, loving atmosphere for our kids. One choice we made was that for family events and large parties at our home, we don't serve alcohol. Some people were really disappointed by that because it represented a change in the way we socialize. We spend time with people we love who do things differently than we do. Our parties seem to end a lot earlier than they used to, we have much more fun, and we never have to worry about designated drivers.

Between the last edition of this book and this one, we were blessed with the birth of our daughter Chloe. In the midst of the book tour I learned I was pregnant with our third child. We were thrilled! The book tour was a wonderful opportunity for me to share with people. It was also a very demanding schedule, on top of mothering and running the business. In my life I only remember calling in sick to work for half a day when I had the stomach flu. With this pregnancy I was exhausted. My first concern was to keep the baby healthy and safe. I was at one of the busiest cycles of my career and I was out there on this book tour telling people about "Powerful Boundaries" and "keeping your priorities in order." Meanwhile, I was too busy to give God, my husband, and our children the time they deserved. Feeling pulled in every direction, I was approaching meltdown. My family and my partners insisted I postpone part of the tour. This was difficult because I felt I would be letting people down after making a commitment, something I try never to do. . . . The pregnancy was a powerful change and has caused me to make more powerful changes in my life. I am blessed that my team continues to support me during this busy and precious time.

On March 12, 2003, Chloe Kathleen Ireland Olsen was born! After a long and full day of labor, Chloe arrived weighing 10 pounds 10 ounces and measuring 21$^{1}/_{2}$ inches long. Both Erik and Lily were excited and eagerly awaited her arrival. Since Chloe's birth came well after Lily's bedtime, her Auntie Baret took her home before she fell asleep in the hospital.

Erik was determined to be with me and Greg for the birth, so my mom kept him with her up by my shoulder. He was so mature and proud of his new baby sister. Chloe came out with this beautiful, interested expression on her face. She made eye contact with everyone and snuggled up in my arms. Chloe is now four and a half months old and has a strong and wonderful personality. Chloe is joyous. She just learned to laugh out loud. She is strong and peaceful, energetic and curious. Chloe has a strong will and I know that it will serve her well. She loves being outdoors and feeling the wind on her face. She enjoyed her first camping trip. She has a beautiful smile that lights up her whole face. When I feel guilty that Chloe will never get the attention an only child receives, I am reminded that Erik and Lily give her is something I cannot give. Her siblings adore her. (Let's hope this continues when she starts talking and getting into their toys!) Lily is always happy to help, bringing diapers, making sure Chloe is happy and comfortable. Erik is happy to hold her and play with her. Chloe is a tremendous joy and blessing to our family. She is certainly a powerful change.

Since becoming parents, our priorities have changed. One of the greatest changes is that as a mother I am taught great lessons of compassion and understanding by my children and their friends.

Little things I would have ignored from my adult perspective—when seen through my children's eyes— seem much larger. These are things like the games my children play, the language used in front of them. I believe we are all role models whether we like it or not. Unless we live in complete isolation, someone is looking to us and observing our behavior. Are they seeing adults behave in a way that enhances respect and dignity or belittles another person. What I once saw as a practical joke, I might now see as an attack on someone's dignity. Walk around in the world from the height and perspective of a child. Things in your life may look rather different. That may cause you to make powerful changes.

It's so easy to get caught up in the day-to-day obligations of life. There's so much pressure, especially on women, to have it all, to do it all, and so much expectation of succeeding. I don't believe it's possible to have it all—whatever that means—but I do believe that it is possible to have enough. For example, making the decision to become a parent is difficult for both the mother and father. I once heard a story about the idea of having it all. It has stuck with me ever since. Not too long ago, I was really giving a lot of thought to what having it all meant personally to me. Our pastor shared a story about a family who had bought a very large, beautiful house. To pay for the house, the father would get up at 4:30 in the morning to drive his two-hour commute to work and he wouldn't get home until 8:00 at night. He'd walk in the door as his kids were going to bed. He did this every day, six days a week—so they could have this "dream house." They indeed had this house, but they did not have what I would call a home.

The biggest changes seem to arrive at the most inopportune times. A sudden death of a loved one, finding yourself out of work, or a divorce are all examples of changes that will never arrive conveniently. Getting fired is the kind of unexpected change that has a tremendous impact on your life. I have been fired from two jobs. Both times it felt like I had failed miserably. The first time I was fired was from a guest appearance on the NBC television series, *Saved by the Bell*. I read the script and I thought that my part was a little silly and I couldn't really connect with my character. I was cast as the school nurse that one of the teenage male characters was supposed to have a crush on. Sometimes, I think *too* much and when I do, I have a hard time. Especially when it comes to acting, and I am supposed to be thinking of, and as, the character I am playing. I start to ask myself a lot of questions and then I end up losing my focus. That's exactly what happened with this job. The director kept telling me to just read the lines. He told me to flirt with the boy. I didn't feel comfortable coming on to a teenager. I knew that it was just a fantasy scene, but I couldn't do it. It just didn't feel right to me. I wasn't a good enough actress to figure out a way to give the director something that would make him happy without compromising my beliefs. The shoot was a disaster! Later that day as I was driving home, I received a call telling me that I had been fired. It was a humbling first. I had been rejected a lot as a model, but never fired. It was a big blow. The pain gave me an incredible opportunity to learn and grow. Being fired was so humbling that one big change for me was that it removed the fear I used to have of auditioning. The rejection process doesn't have anywhere near the impact of getting a job and losing it. The ironic twist to this story is that although I was fired by NBC on that show, a few years later the network offered me television movies, and my Christmas projects are on PAX, which is part of the NBC family. In life and in business, history doesn't change. Perspectives do. Today when I act it usually needs to fulfill our mission statement of finding solutions for families, especially busy moms. Earlier this year I had the opportunity to play an expectant mother diagnosed with colon cancer on the Lifetime series *Strong Medicine*. It was a wonderful experience because we were able to bring attention to the importance of early detection, especially in women. My work at KIWW focuses on serving our customers. Acting is a cherished interest but not my primary focus. That's a change in my life and career that is truly powerful.

Another powerful change . . . While we were working on this book, Kmart filed for Chapter 11 bankruptcy. Fortunately, they have since emerged. At the time, family, friends, people in the media—all wanted to know my feelings. My first concern was for the hundreds of thousands of employees and the shareholders. Kmart is a legendary company. I will always be grateful for the opportunity that the corporation and its management team provided to us. I was reminded that from the beginning of my business, I believed in diversification so that one can weather the winds of change. Even though the majority of our business is with retailers outside of Kmart, as a Kmart shareholder, associate, and shopper, I hope and pray for the very best.

My mom is the most positive person I know. She is an expert at seeing the cup as half full. When I was younger, she used to say that "an optimist is someone who wakes up and says, 'Good morning, Lord' and a pessimist is someone who wakes up and says, 'Good Lord, it's morning.'" My dad instilled a belief in me that I could do anything. He said that I could be president if I wanted it badly enough. My dad really loves his daughters! With the innocence of a child, I believed him. By giving me that kind of hope, my father helped me have a no-limits way of thinking. That was truly a blessing. My parents each allowed me to fail and succeed on my own. I developed my sense of independence as a result of that kind of upbringing and that has helped me in every area of my life.

One way that I deal with change most effectively is to surround myself with people who love and support me. Please do that for yourself. You deserve it. One day before I left for an audition, I was telling my husband that I didn't think I stood a chance of getting the particular part I was going out for. I knew that the director was seeing so many actresses with much more experience. I was feeling insecure. My husband listened to me go on and on about my fears and why the director would never choose me. Then he said three words that changed my whole perspective and re-ignited the passion I had felt as young girl. He said, "Why not you?" He stopped me cold. He was right! I had stopped dreaming the big dream. Earlier in this chapter I talked of my father's belief that I could do anything. You'd expect that with accomplishments, belief in yourself grows. Not necessarily. As my business career grew, the actor in me felt less confident than ever. I wasn't auditioning with the same frequency. I wasn't studying. I've never been a strong actress to begin with. But it is something I love to do. I was allowing my fear of failure to push me back into my cold protective shell instead of enjoying the process. I wasn't taking a risk, which meant I couldn't be disappointed but I also couldn't experience a powerful change. I had come up with every reason imaginable why I wouldn't get the part—that I didn't have enough experience, I wasn't good enough, I was too shy, whatever. I never considered the option that I would get the role. Greg told me that I had to go into the audition like he approaches surfing. He takes charge with a fearless go-for-it attitude when he's in the ocean. He taught me that when you're in the line-up and a good wave comes your way, as long as you're not cutting somebody off, you must go for it. Even if you fall on your face it's better to try and fail than let the possibility slip away. That kind of thinking is very motivational.

The audition was for the Pulitzer Prize–winning play *Three Tall Women* written by Edward Albee. It was a serious play. I very much wanted to be in the cast. Stephen Roseberry, one of my business partners at Sterling-Winters Company, faced many obstacles in getting me the audition. He has always been a fearless leader when it comes to my work. To know that someone believes in you is extremely empowering. Stephen always bulldozes down doors to find exciting new options for me. I was shocked and touched by his strong faith in me and in his belief that I had the ability to be in that play. I decided if Stephen believed in me enough to stick his neck out and put his own reputation on the line, then the least I could do was try my best. Before the audition, I spent many hours working with Rick Mokler—a wonderful acting teacher and friend in Santa Barbara. Once again, surrounding myself with people who unconditionally support and love me made a difference. Greg's "Why not you?" and Stephen's faith in me gave me faith in myself. That confidence is what got me the part.

Once I was cast, I faced a dilemma. There was a line in the play that required me to take the Lord's name in vain. There are many great groups who lobby for the rights of others. But who's lobbying for Jesus? It's got to be the people who love Him. I'm one of those people. Because of my beliefs, I simply couldn't do it. Stephen had worked so hard to get me the audition, and I really wanted the job. I approached the brilliant director, Glyn O'Malley, about changing the line. He explained that Mr. Albee "changes dialogue for no one." Every word he writes has such profound meaning. It was a large conflict for me so I spoke to Mom about my dilemma. She reminded me that God is a God of peace. If I didn't feel peace in my decision, then it was not God's will. Well, that was that. As

Christians, we must stand up for Jesus. I couldn't go through with the play because I simply was not at peace taking the Lord's name in vain.

I ask God that His will be done in my life every single day. If I truly want Him to be in charge of all things, then I must trust that His will is the answer, and I do. After Glyn thought about my dilemma, he changed my performance to honor the Lord in prayer. He altered my character to be a Christian and her line would be said as a prayer. That was a very powerful change that brought me tremendous peace and allowed me to joyously play the part. It was an amazing experience and in the end, everyone was comfortable with the change including Edward Albee, who complimented the entire production. That peace reminded me what it feels like to have serenity in my life and what it feels like when I don't. It brought a calmness to me, and the turmoil was gone. It was so easy once I made my decision. The answer was right in front of me the whole time.

I had the best time doing the show and I learned a great deal working with wonderfully talented people. It was great to play this character. I made new discoveries every day—about myself, my ability to stretch as an actress, and about my own capability to change. *Three Tall Women* taught me so much and it had a wonderful and positive impact on everything else I have done as an actress since. Those words my mother spoke to me that day have so much truth. I think about her advice in all of the decisions I have made since. If I don't feel peace about something then it is not God's will. Ask yourself the same question next time you're facing a crisis. Will you feel at peace with your decision? If the answer is no, then it's not the right change to make in your life.

Change can be positive or negative. Even changes disguised as challenges are often wonderful opportunities for personal progress. It's so important to work through negativity and discover what life lessons are there for us. Two people who face the same set of challenges will probably choose to handle the situation in entirely different ways. One person may allow that circumstance to destroy their plan, and the other will figure out a way to triumphantly emerge from the situation having grown and built character along the way. Taking risk is important. In the end, if the experience was good, it was worth it. I have a friend who recently went through a change in her business. She decided to break away from her partner to start a new business for herself. Though she was frightened of being on her own, it was really the best thing that could have happened to her. She has established a company that is fast becoming the top in its field, something she would never have been able to do

had she stayed in her old association. Her former situation was tiring and draining in every way. She had
hit a plateau and wasn't able to make the changes
necessary to make that company work. On the other
hand, there was stability in being a part of an established company. My friend couldn't see the positive
possibilities of being on her own until she broke away
from the comfort zone she had been in in her business
partnership. The scariest change turned out to be the
most positive and powerful change.

Oftentimes, change is something that happens *to*
us. However, when we initiate positive change, that is
truly powerful. While it is comfortable and encouraging to spend our time with people who think like we
do, if we only associate with people who agree with us
we will never be able to accomplish positive change.
Before becoming a parent I said I would never expose
my future children to certain children's stories where
good behavior was portrayed by characters physically
looking one way and bad behavior was portrayed
by characters who physically looked another way.
Perhaps my modeling background heightened my
sensitivity to this issue.

When the children entered our lives I did ease up
a bit, but this matter became very concerning to me
when Lily received a princess book that she absolutely
adored. Children love repetition and she wanted

me to read it again and again and again. Not only did the stories in this book have good and bad behavior represented by certain physicalities, but the princesses behaved like victims and made some obvious bad choices. As I read the stories Lily was begging for I did not feel peace. Not until we made some changes. We refer to this as "Empowering the Princesses." We altered the stories to have the Princess make different choices than those that were originally written for her. These changes in her attitude and behavior cause her situation and outcome to be much more positive than in the fairy-tale conclusion. Instead of allowing a stranger in her home and eating poisoned food from this person, the Princess uses her words and when that fails, she dials 9-1-1. Rather than bring the Princess back to life with a kiss, the Prince hears laughter and music coming from the cottage. The Princess and her seven friends are celebrating the fact that this person with bad intentions was having a long time-out in jail. After spending time getting to know each other and discovering that they shared similar core values and enjoyed each other's company, the Prince and Princess fall in love and get married. As I experience the impact of this story on Lily's behavior I am reminded that this is a powerful change.

The key to successfully dealing with changes is learning from each experience. Find something won-

derful, terrific, inspiring, great, exciting, dynamic; just
find something in it that is good. You have to keep
your eye on the big picture, even if it isn't apparent to
you at the moment. Knowing that God never gives us
more than we can handle is one way that I manage my
own concerns about change. It's essential to not let
fear hold you back. It is essential to see the seed of
equal or greater benefit in every adversity, challenge,
or change. Like it or not, change forces us to move
from our comfort zone, which in turn challenges us to
take needed risks . . . to take a leap of faith.

Relationship changes, career changes, having
children, making difficult decisions that require deep
thought and concentration on the outcome, all deal
with actions and reactions. I take that into consider-
ation when dealing with change. I ask powerful questions to help me understand the purpose of change.
Why is this happening? What am I supposed to be
learning from this? Who will be affected by this
change? Do I have peace about this?

My business partners, Erik, Jason, Jon, Stephen,
and Steve, have each helped all of us deal with the
everyday changes that we encounter in our business.
There have been many changes when it comes to my
relationships. When I'm working with different
strategic partners, I invest that time to get to know
them, for them to get to know us, and to really

understand what our vision is. This takes a lot of work and time. It's important for everyone to understand how we can work together, how I want to be a part of the team, the big picture. In professional situations, people move on in their careers, and you have a whole new set of executives, and the process begins all over again, but many times those changes, unbeknownst to us, turn out to our benefit. They can be good—they cause us to grow and reach new levels of accomplishment.

Sometimes, when my schedule gets to a point of overload, I unintentionally put God on the back burner. I simply don't have enough hours in the day for one extra moment of prayer or serenity. That's when I find that everything seems to fall out of balance. I feel less close to God, but not because He's moved away from me—He's always there, but because I've moved away from Him. When I put God first and make enough time for Him, everything shifts back into place. It is so easy to forget that He must be the priority, no matter what else is going on in my life. My faith has pulled me through every tough challenge I have faced and every unexpected change that has come my way. It's great to have goals, but it's important as we experience changes that we don't forget to enjoy the journey. Being content is enjoying each step of the way, whatever that may be. Regardless of the changes we're going through, as difficult as they are, we can take heart in knowing that changes are powerful.

LESSON FIVE

Change is the only certainty in life.

* Change forces us out of our comfort zone.

* Celebrate positive changes. Work through negative ones to discover something positive in them.

* When God is on the back burner, everything falls out of balance.

* Why not you?

* Don't let fear hold you back.

* Keep your eye on the big picture.

* It's great to have goals, but don't forget to enjoy the journey.

* Growth means preparing for change.

* Prepare for change. It will happen.

* History doesn't change. Perspectives do.

Chapter Six

POWERFUL
FINANCIAL WISDOM

◈ ◈

Inspiration

BLESSED IS THE MAN WHO FINDS
WISDOM, THE MAN WHO GAINS
UNDERSTANDING, FOR HE IS MORE
PROFITABLE THAN SILVER AND YIELDS
BETTER RETURNS THAN GOLD.

Proverbs 3:13

Each of us has, is, or will experience financial difficulties at some point in our lives. That's the nature of life. Financial independence has always been important to me, because of the freedom that it provides. I never want to be forced into making a decision out of financial desperation. I certainly never lacked for anything important. Though my family instilled a sense of financial responsibility in me at a young age, I didn't always practice powerful financial wisdom.

As a child I saw abuse of money, and it scared me. My father's job required him to mediate and negotiate on behalf of people who, from my young perspective, were frequently being mistreated. Seeing individuals oppressed by others made me fear wealth and power. When I was a little girl, my father's favorite movie was *Robin Hood*. The rich people in the film, like the corporate executives my dad dealt with, seemed so bad, and it really frightened me. I began thinking that perhaps it was bad to have money.

I wasn't always the saver that I have become, but I have always worked and earned my own money. Out of necessity, I learned about financial responsibility at an early age. From the day I went after my paper route, I understood that I might be challenged about being seen as an equal in business. I never wanted the man in my life to tell me that I could or could not do anything I wanted because he controlled the money. I refused to be in the position of having to depend on anyone for something as important as financial support. If I wanted something, I'd go after it myself. My dad used to tell us the story of how he saved his money as a teenager, and it inspired me. He was originally saving his money to buy a really snazzy car he wanted. He ended up using his savings for a down payment on his first house. I always knew that I wanted to have my own financial security and independence. I also knew that it was possible.

As a young girl, if I wanted to do something, I would figure out a way to make it happen. When I was little, like most siblings, there came a time when I decided that I no longer wanted to share a bedroom with my older sister. Unbeknownst to my parents, I called a contractor. I had him come to our house and bid on the cost of converting our garage into an extra room. I had my job delivering newspapers in our neighborhood, and I figured that I could pay for the work with my carrier wages. I did the math, and even if I saved every penny I was making, it would have taken me years to pay for the work, so that didn't quite work out as I had hoped. Eventually, when my sister Mary moved away from home, I did get my own room. It was a real blessing that I didn't have things handed to me growing up.

I was an okay model. I was never the highest paid or the top choice in the business. I had a really good start and was able to work as often as I wanted. In the beginning, it actually cost me more money to buy one of those Italian *Vogue* magazines to get the tear sheets for my portfolio than I made shooting the photos. Some people may think that I made a lot of money being on the cover of magazines, but it simply wasn't the case. What I had were very good relationships that helped me work on a regular basis. As I shared with you, I worked with a wonderful photographer, Peter Lindberg, who would arrange for me to fly to Europe once a month for a shoot that helped me build my résumé and gain much-needed experience. Once I started working in New York, I did more editorial work. After I paid my agency fees and taxes, the money went pretty quickly. I established myself as a reliable model, so I started to get booked for advertising and catalogue work. I did very little runway work. I was too uncoordinated to walk in the high heels. I have small feet for my height, so I never felt like I had the proper leverage for my five-foot-eleven-inch body. I feared tipping over. I was also terribly embarrassed to change in front of everybody. It just wasn't fun for me, and so I never seriously pursued that part of the business.

When I was chosen to work with *Sports Illustrated* it was a great job, but at the time, while it was very visible all over the world, it was not considered prestigious in the fashion industry. It wasn't like doing *Vogue*. I felt so much more comfortable doing *Sports Illustrated* than I did *Vogue*. The shoots didn't have that high-fashion feel. Jule Campbell is so down to earth and she always treated everyone like family. Ultimately, it was the cover of *Sports Illustrated* that put me in another category as a model. But I knew for sure that would be a fleeting phase of my career.

During my modeling career, women like Paulina Porizkova, Elle McPherson, Kim Alexis, and Carol Alt were all considered the top models in the business. It was an interesting time in fashion because the super-model era was just beginning with beautiful girls like Cindy Crawford, Linda Evangelista, Naomi Campbell, and Claudia Schiffer, all of whom were just starting out. On the other hand, whether I liked it or not, modeling was the source of my income. I realize now that if something happened that prevented me from working, I was not as prepared as I should have been.

A few months before my twenty-fifth birthday, Greg and I decided to go skiing with some of our friends in Telluride, Colorado. I am a pretty good skier, but I lack style and grace. I was trying to go down a mogul run, showing off for Greg, when I caught an edge of my ski and flipped over. I heard a *pop*. I knew I had blown out my knee. I was taken down the mountain on a sled, in too much pain to feel the humiliation. I had a couple of surgeries to place pins in my knee and ended up in a cast for two and a half months. When the cast finally came off, my leg was skinny, very white, and very hairy! My doctor said I couldn't shave my leg for two weeks because the skin was too soft and tender. I never noticed how much my legs were like my dad's until the day the cast came off. Afterward, I wasn't feeling very feminine. I knew there wouldn't be a lot of modeling opportunities until I recovered. My skiing accident came at a time where missing the work I had always complained about created financial challenges.

While recovering from the accident, I spent my emergency fund and needed money for mortgage payments and other living expenses. I'd never realized

the importance of a credit rating. I was self-employed.
I had bought a condo. I was feeling pretty secure.
Once again in an instant, life changed. Banks were
reluctant to loan money to a model on crutches
with a hairy leg. Finally, and fortunately, a finance
company agreed to loan me some money until I was
back on my feet. While I appreciated being able to
pay my bills with the much-needed loan, it impressed
upon me the importance of living beneath my means.
The interest rate was very steep, and with each payment I realized had I been as thrifty as possible, I
wouldn't have been in that situation.

I knew that I had a finite amount of time before I
would be quickly replaced by the up-and-coming stars
of the business. I wasn't living an extravagant
lifestyle, so after my skiing accident, I was able to start
saving a good portion of my income. Many people
believe that living within or slightly above their
means is justifiable. Not me. Since my accident, my
approach toward powerful financial wisdom is simple.
Live slightly below your means, and you will always
have enough money to live. My philosophy is that
you have to find the things in your life that make
you happy rather than believing that money will solve
all of your problems—because it won't. Money can
create comfort and it will create opportunity, but if
you're in an unhealthy place emotionally, having

money can give you more problems—not resolve the ones you have.

It's ironic that I needed an injury to turn a concept I had grown up with into a real life lesson. I always understood the value of a dollar and the satisfaction of having my own money. When I was in the third grade, I remember being called to the principal's office. I was really scared because I was basically a pretty good kid and I had never been to the principal's office before. I thought that I must have done something wrong, but I didn't know what. When I got to his office, instead of being scolded for something, I was congratulated for doing so well on my money-counting project.

As my career got busier, I realized I needed professional advice to help me with my finances. My friend, accountant, and business manager, Peter Mainstain and his partners at Tanner, Mainstain Hoffer & Peyrot have been an important part of my life for more than twenty years. Peter and his wife, Leslie, and their family are a special part of our lives. Just after my twenty-first birthday, I was able to buy my own condominium in Malibu. That was amazing to me, because most of my friends were just buying their first cars. I didn't know anyone my age who'd been able to buy their first home. My mom said that the first time she saw me swimming in the pool at my condo was the first time she can recall that I wasn't swimming just for fun. I was swimming to stay fit because I had a mortgage to pay. Now that my paycheck is no longer dependent upon my appearance (thank goodness!), I'm back to swimming just for fun.

Women especially need to understand finances and to have their own financial independence. It's great to have a husband who can support you and your family, but don't depend on it. You might *choose* to support your family, you may *have* to. Learning to be financially savvy will help you be prepared for the future, regardless of the obstacles that may come along. There are so many simple ways to accomplish this.

It might mean making your own money and keeping it separate from your husband's. Maybe it means saving a little out of the weekly allowance and putting it away in your own account. Establish your own credit separate from your spouse. Open a bank account in only your name. Joint accounts are great, but it's a good idea to have a safer place to keep your extra spending money than the kitchen cookie jar. If you're married, decide whether you can handle financial issues together. If not, choose the person best suited to the discipline that is required. Support the decision you've made. Whoever handles all the finances, you need to know where you are financially at all times and where all of your assets are kept. Bank accounts, bonds, stocks, even if the money is hidden under the rug in the living room—know where all of the family assets are located. If you don't have a credit card in your own name, get one. Also, be aware of any liabilities such as loans, credit card debt, mortgages, taxes, and other financial obligations. There may be a day when something happens, and you find that you are suddenly on your own, perhaps for the first time.

Over the years, I have gained financial wisdom by practicing the importance of saving and investing. I really learned to start saving as a child. As a young entrepreneur, I decided that I would save twenty dollars a month from my paper route and implemented this plan. I practiced this monthly ritual for the three and a half years that I was a carrier. When I retired from the route, I had a wonderful savings account. That savings provided me with the luxury of taking a month off before starting a new job. It also made it possible for me to purchase my first car three years later. A percentage of every dollar you earn should be put away for yourself. Financial advisors suggest trying to put away 10 percent of your paycheck into some kind of savings vehicle. If you can't put 10 percent of your earnings away at this moment, make an effort to put *something* into your savings. Little by little, you

will be saving enough money to help out in an emergency or unexpected crisis. It's important to invest
and save for an emergency fund.

Discover the miracle of compounded interest.
Take small amounts of money over a period of time
and watch how they grow. The benefit of compounded interest is something that is available to
everyone no matter what your financial situation.
First, take care of your absolute financial obligations,
such as tithing, taxes, and other necessities of living.
Then pay yourself. This is important whether you're
dealing with a little bit of money or a lot. There is so
much information available on compounded interest.
Check with your bank, local library, bookstore, and
even the Internet to research options that may be
right for you. The time you spend on this research is a
worthy investment.

Once savings become a part of your budget, you
will become more realistic about what you can and
can't afford. Some of the best advice I was given about
saving is, when it comes to investing, diversify. I
believe in diversification—not only in business but
also in savings. Diversify wherever you can in equity,
real estate, and cash. That way, when life's uncertainties happen, you will have something to protect you
and your loved ones.

Try to save as much as you can for retirement

whether it is an IRA or a company-sponsored plan. If you need assistance in finding a plan, seek professional advisors who will help define a financial strategy that is right for you and your family.

How many credit cards do you have? Do you really need all of them? I have found that, with fewer lines of credit, most of us are better able to stay within our spending budget and are less likely to find ourselves in debt. I have learned to shop for the best interest rates. Many working people don't realize that banks will negotiate credit card–interest rates or even the interest on your existing rate. Transferring balances from other cards is an incentive many banks use to lower their rates and keep you as a customer. If you find that during hard times you can't pay your bills, talk to your bank, creditors, and lenders. They can work out payment plans that you can adhere to and help you through those challenging financial times.

When you are spending money, ask yourself if this is something that will appreciate in value or depreciate in value. If it is something like a car that is going to depreciate, think twice about the amount of money you are willing to put into it. Are you spending money in places that are building assets or simply giving you cancelled checks? When it comes to buying a home, choose the least expensive home in the best neighborhood. When it comes to a car, leasing is often a good option for a business situation, though buying may be better in a personal situation. I recommend buying a car that will safely get you from point A to point B. It's important to remember that an expensive car usually means expensive maintenance and expensive insurance. Don't get caught up in spending money you don't have to impress people you might not even like. Sometimes people will spend money on a fancy car and forgo important things like health insurance.

Investigate different insurance options, whether it is homeowners, health, or even auto. What kind is possible? Many agencies offer discounts for people with better credit ratings. If your credit needs cleaning up, take care of it. Make that a priority. It will save you a lot of money in the long run.

If you have children, it is important to plan for their education early. This doesn't mean that your children shouldn't work to contribute to the costs, but the earlier you start, the more options there will be. Set up a compound-interest savings account in their name. Do this as early as possible. See if your student qualifies for student loans. There are so many opportunities available to help with the high cost of education. Don't let financial stress be the reason your son or daughter doesn't have a chance at seeking higher education.

While I don't want to encourage people not to help others, be wise and help to the degree you can afford. When it comes to loaning money be discerning and don't be afraid to say no. This doesn't make you a bad person. If you do decide to loan someone money, be sure that it's money you can say goodbye to. For me it was interesting that I was much more financially responsible when I had less money. When the larger paychecks started coming in, I stopped planning for my future in the way that I used to, I stopped taking money off the top and putting away in my emergency fund. It was easy to forget the basics. Lifestyle can gobble up income, creating the illusion of living a life of prosperity instead of real prosperity. Don't try to get rich quick. Slow and steady savings are the best methods for long-term financial stability. That's something that everybody ought to do no matter how much money you make. That was a really powerful lesson.

Now, more than ever before, women need to take care of themselves financially. Building your own savings is a simple defense against life's uncertainties. And take it from someone who knows, life is never certain.

As a CEO, I have discovered that it is very challenging to finance the entrepreneurial vision. I can't think of anything that has helped me in my business life more than learning not to be afraid of money and understanding its place and its priorities. It's important to acknowledge the good that money can do and the blessings that can help so many people's lives. But it's not about what we have or what we don't have, it's where our hearts are, and that is what's really important. Our son, Erik, shares his name with three very special men. His great-grandfather, my cousin, and my business partner, Erik Sterling—who is Uncle Erik to my kids. Erik does a tremendous amount of work operating our company. I am awed by the way he handles the business of our business. He is a man of few words. When he does speak, it is profound. I can always see the wheels turning—even if he doesn't articulate his thoughts to me right away. The name Erik means leader. As I watch my son grow, I am honored that he shares the same traits. They are both secure, adventurous, strong, and have a great sense of joy and compassion.

Shortly after I started working with Sterling-Winters Company, Erik accompanied me to a meeting. They reassured me that it didn't matter whether I earned money right away. Erik's advice was that if I did quality work, the money would come. Throughout my career, I had never heard someone speak like that. He was so confident that the money would come if it wasn't our main focus. I felt guilty for taking up his time and for not being a big money earner for the company. His words gave me hope and helped restore my faith in people. Without Erik Sterling, there would be no Kathy Ireland brand. He personally invested in the company and made sacrifices without ever telling me. I never would have let him had I known at the time. Erik is a very fair man and a very tough negotiator. I greatly respect the coexistence of those qualities. His faith in me allowed us to work together and accomplish amazing things. Erik demonstrates tremendous support in our lives in areas outside of our business association. It is a dream of mine along with a group of parents to open a Christian school for children. Erik is of the Jewish faith. His interest in helping me see that dream become a reality presses upon my heart the true meaning of Christianity. That kind of love is so rare. It reminds me of another Jewish man who reached out to all people regardless of their background. That man was God's son, Jesus. Jesus was a strong leader motivated by love. Erik's wisdom in the financial aspects of my business has helped me become a stronger businessperson. His guidance and sincerity have helped me to succeed in ways I could never have imagined. Through his own way of operating, Erik has also demonstrated and taught me how to measure success in ways that aren't financial.

I am truly grateful for the peace of mind I have as a CEO. All of my team members work together to see to it that Kathy Ireland WorldWide runs like a well-oiled machine. Let's face it, if I didn't want to run a profitable company, I'd devote all of my time to being a stay-at-home mom and doing nonprofit work. I enjoy running a profitable company. My whole life, from the day I painted my first rocks to the day I started selling socks, whenever I thought about profit in business, I always talked in terms of net profit. I make sure that everyone is paid what they are owed. Overhead, commissions, taxes, and other expenditures are factored in before I calculate income. Also, giving back to God is extremely important. All of our blessings come from God. Honoring Him with the first fruits of our labors is a special joy. Tithing is an honor. God doesn't need our money, but He knows what we need. If we trust in Him, He will provide for us.

I have such respect for people who are content. My husband and I have friends who have figured out how to be content with very few material possessions. They work, but it's merely a justification to travel and surf. They love the freedom of their lives, and they are not unhappy that they don't have more possessions. To me that's the key to happiness. You have to love what you do and appreciate who you are. Most of the things I like to do are free. Most of our family outings as a kid involved doing things that cost nothing, such as hiking or spending the day at the beach, a tradition I have continued with my own children.

As a parent, I want to instill my sense and sensibility about financial freedom and wisdom in my children. I have put enough money aside to help pay for my kids' education, but they will need to find their own way in life. I feel that giving them all of the things that come with too much money will only bring on a set of problems that could otherwise be avoided. Granted, my kids are being raised differently than my husband and I were raised. They certainly have some material advantages, but they are not being raised in a pampered way.

Just before the holidays last year, Erik told me that he wanted a Play Station 2 and a puppy for Christmas. I explained to him that it seemed like a pretty tall order for Santa to bring both and I didn't want him to be upset if he didn't get everything he wanted. He understood and came up with a plan to start a dog-sitting business in the neighborhood to earn his own money so that he could buy the Play Station. He decided that he was going to put posters up all over our town advertising his dog-sitting services. I thought it was great that he took the initiative to earn his own money. Before Erik could get his business off the ground, Santa came and sure enough, brought him the Play Station and a brand new puppy. That morning, after opening his gifts, I realized that by Santa giving him everything he asked for, his motivation could be lost. It's so important that we allow our children the opportunity to grow, learn from their mistakes and realize that they are capable of so much. I never want to give them all the material things they want and rob them of their motivation. Too much money can unbalance the scale. I have seen kids being raised with no boundaries, responsibility, or appreciation for the luxuries of their daily lives. I want my children to know the value of a dollar, and that can sometimes be difficult to accomplish. There are certain things expected of our children simply for being part of the family, like picking up after themselves. Erik, who is a little older and can handle more responsibility, now has additional chores, like setting the table and caring for his dog, Sparky, for which he earns an allowance. I believe it is important for children to have the opportunity to earn their own money—that is theirs to do with as they wish. They need to learn to save, and they also need to be allowed to make some financial mistakes that they can learn from. Erik understands the idea of earning his allowance, but he did question me the other day as to why he had to make his bed when I don't always make mine. I explained to him that when he grows up and makes his own money, if he can afford to, he could have someone make his bed!

While money can be a great luxury, it can some-

times compromise values and standards we set for ourselves. For me, especially when it comes to business, if
I think something I do will disappoint someone or
challenge my personal beliefs, I will weigh the options
long and hard before I agree to decline or decide to
continue a relationship. It's a constant process of eval-
uation as I grow and learn. After one year of working
with Anheuser Busch, I decided not to renew my contract. Anheuser Busch is a wonderful company that
gives generously to many good organizations. They
agreed to put a generous amount of money toward their
"Know When to Say When" campaign. While for
some people this relationship would not be wrong, I
simply didn't feel continuing with them was the right
choice for me. It was a secure income that I kept telling
myself was going to be a good nest egg. But deep down,
it didn't sit quite right with me. I wasn't at peace. I had
witnessed the perils of alcohol abuse on families. Some
people can drink responsibly and others simply cannot
control their drinking. I talked about how I felt with
one of my business partners who has been and
continues to be in alcohol recovery. Though my work
wouldn't have inspired him to take a drink, it still
didn't feel right to me. Deciding to walk away from
renewing my contract was a serious decision, because
financially it was extremely valuable and it was at a
time in my life where I had no other certain income.

As I thought about it, I started to recognize that alcohol has had a negative impact on people I love over the years. I no longer felt comfortable promoting a product that has caused so much pain for so many families either by alcohol abuse, drunk driving, or other drinking/health-related issues. I made the decision to move on, and my business partners were stunned. They asked me what I planned to do for money? I told them that I was healthy and capable and I could do anything. I knew that I would be fine. I don't have fears about my economic future. My beliefs were stronger than any possible downside to not renewing the contract. I had nothing else going on, but I knew I'd made the right move for me. I felt that peace. Six weeks after I made my decision, I got involved in a partnership with Moretz Mills to create my brand of socks. That was the beginning of Kathy Ireland WorldWide. Had I maintained the prior relationship, KIWW might never have happened. I had faith that God would provide.

There is a passage in the Bible that says, "It is easier for a camel to go through the eye of a needle than for a rich man to pass into the kingdom of God." I talked at length with my pastor about my fear and guilt, and he explained to me that having money is not a sin, but it was the love of money that's a sin. You can have no money but love it, and that is far worse than having it and not loving it. You may own money, but you must never let it own you. There's a lot of responsibility that comes with having money, and I believe God gives all of us great opportunities. Different people choose different paths where money is involved. When those choices are based in integrity and honor, whether we have a little or a lot, we can do God's will.

LESSON SIX

Live beneath your means, and you will always have enough money.

- Each one of us has, is, or will experience financial difficulties in our lives.

- Financial independence is important.

- Money can create comfort and opportunity—nothing more.

- Money won't solve all your problems.

- Own money; never let it own you.

- Having money is not a sin; loving money is.

Chapter Seven

POWERFUL BELIEFS
AND BOUNDARIES

❖ ❖

Inspiration
WHEN A FLOOD CAME,
THE TORRENT STRUCK THAT HOUSE
BUT COULD NOT SHAKE IT,
BECAUSE IT WAS WELL BUILT.
Luke 6:4–8

I live a pretty normal life. I take my kids to school, I'm involved in the local community. I am on the school board. I take Lily to ballet and Erik to all of his different sporting events. I go to church and teach Sunday school. I work. I'm not so different than any other busy mom. The work I do may be different, but inside, you and I share more similarities than differences. I believe building my brand has helped me have a better understanding of what women want. I think that when women are busy, many of their daily duties fall by the wayside. That's the reason I have been so adamant about setting boundaries in my life that coincide with my beliefs. That's the only way I can think of to protect my time with my family and to allow myself to chill out from time to time. I can get pretty immersed in my job as a CEO or my job as a stay-at-home mom. Let's face it, moms are the CEOs of their families. When I am home, I want to be 100 percent there. I fight for balance, so that I am with my family much more than I am away from them. I've come to understand that when I take a vacation, I want to enjoy myself. My partners sometimes decide to work through theirs. I have to remind myself to take a step back and let people do what makes them happy. If my partners enjoy working those kinds of hours, more power to them. I admire it. I respect it. But I have certain boundaries that work for me. I know they admire and respect those as well.

I learned about standing up for what I believe in from an early age—it never bothers me that my beliefs may be against the tide. When I was a child, I remember attending rallies where Cesar Chavez spoke. Dad worked with Mr. Chavez to help improve conditions for the farm workers. My mom, sisters, and I marched with Dad in various demonstrations. I will never forget walking with all of those people who shared an incredible strength for a common goal. Knowing what is right for you in your own life will help lead you to be successful in any endeavor. I encourage you to figure out your values ahead of time so you won't find yourself in a compromising situation and not know what to do.

Part of my beliefs is creating and setting boundaries that I have the courage to live by. Having boundaries helps me to have that sought-after and important balance each of us strives for in our lives. If we don't believe in ourselves and understand our own value, our boundaries won't protect us. That's what they are in place for. As a parent, I set boundaries for my children all the time. It's a way to protect them. Boundaries are different than setting limits. I want my kids to know that they are limitless in their potential. The same is true for adults. Although boundaries change as our lives do, sticking to them is important. When that photographer wanted me to take my top off, I knew it wasn't something I wanted to do. I knew that it was possible to succeed without ever having to compromise myself. I stuck to the boundaries I had set for myself. Throughout this book I hope I have communicated the importance of setting boundaries in life. It is a mechanism to assure great peace in our lives.

Paul Newman and I have co-chaired a series of fundraising events to prevent drug abuse. Some of the proceeds benefited the Scott Newman Foundation. Scott was Paul's son who died tragically from a drug overdose. He had been through incredible battles with addiction. Paul is a very inspiring man to be around because of his great gentleness, charm, and kindness. He is clearly committed to raising money and awareness in the war on drug abuse. It is that commitment that made it possible for him to co-chair our events and it is the importance of that cause that allows me comfort in talking about the time we spent together. He is a very private man. You immediately recognized that he was being polite and charming, but it was inspirational to see him handle people the way he does. He reaches out and at the same time he carries himself in a way where he maintains a quiet dignity and strength so that people don't intrude beyond a level that is comfortable. He was there for his cause. He showed his support. He did everything that was asked of him, but it was clear that he was someone that you wanted to treat with respect. Not because he is a legendary movie star, which of course he is, but because of his beliefs and the boundaries he had set as a human being. Even though we meet on occasion and have always enjoyed very warm communication, I honor those boundaries as well. He inspires me to recognize and live by my own beliefs and boundaries.

Beliefs and boundaries can be wide ranging. For example, when I am focused on my family time, I will screen phone calls at home. I'm certain that this may seem selfish but because that time is precious it's a boundary I need. There are also boundaries that allow me to be myself in any situation. It took awhile to develop some of those. Years ago, I had been invited to a party to honor Clint Eastwood. I was a vegetarian at the time and the dinner consisted of multiple courses of non-vegetarian fare. We were seated at a fancy table with a floor length tablecloth, and I thought that I was being very clever by stashing each course I couldn't eat in my napkin and tossing it under the table. As dinner came to an end, someone suggested that the dogs, which had been kept separate from the diners, come out to say hello to the guests. They made a mad dash for my chair. They flipped up the tablecloth, and there I was caught with a napkin full of uneaten meat at my feet. I was beyond embarrassed. My table manners have improved since then, and I'm no longer a vegetarian. Today I realize that I have the comfort with my beliefs and boundaries to simply be honest. I could have politely explained my dietary restrictions and declined what I couldn't eat. I was trying once again to fit in. My boundaries were less clear back then. Wise people constantly discover what they believe.

We are all constantly dealing with beliefs and boundaries. There are many people who expect that in order to accomplish an agenda, you have to compromise a belief or boundary. A small infraction here, a rule twist there—the thinking is, who would know? All of the things that I deal with in my life start with my love of the Lord. If a situation doesn't fit with my understanding of God's will, then it crosses a boundary or belief that I have set for myself.

My appearance on *Politically Incorrect* was the first time my pro-life views became public in a national way. People warned me that I was placing my work in a dangerous situation from a publicity standpoint. There was tremendous concern over the possibility of offending people—especially customers. Let's just say that I received a lot of encouragement to pass on the invitation to appear. One of my business partners came to see me and said that if one woman contemplating an abortion watched the show and decided to change her mind as a result of my beliefs, then who cares if the business goes down the drain? He was so right. It was a truly remarkable experience. I was definitely confronted on my beliefs, but that was fine. My desire to speak out for the unborn made that evening meaningful.

Some of the nonprofit organizations that I choose to work with help people who are living with HIV and AIDS. I received letters from some people criticizing my support. I am aware that I will never please everyone, and the truth is, I don't want to. It's an awful place to be—trying to make everyone else happy. In my heart, my goal is to serve God. I know this life isn't just about me or me being happy, even though I feel blessed to have a lot in my life to be happy about. There's a much bigger picture than that.

While setting boundaries is important, sometimes breaking them is even more crucial. The first Kathy Ireland LPGA golf tournament was a very special day, but it was clouded by negative feelings and harsh criticism from people who had a certain set of boundaries and beliefs that were not consistent with my own. My goal was to help bolster the women who play on the LPGA circuit. I have always been a supporter of women's athletics, especially since Lily and Chloe's birth. I think many women athletes are great role models. I'd like to help create more opportunities for female athletes and see to it that the purses are adequate. The women's pay scale in sports is still so much lower than the men's. This is shocking discrimination when you're dealing with world-class athletes. They're warriors in their fields. They have such good, strong spirits, and I think it's essential to honor their achievements and shatter the unfair boundaries set for them. For the golf tournament, I had originally asked if we could host it at Pebble Beach because the Ladies Professional Golf Association has never been allowed to play there. The answer was no. That's someone else's boundary I'd like to break through some day.

One of the reasons I chose to share my thoughts with you in this book is because of the reality that so many people are afraid of Christians. For many,

their only experience with Christianity is what
they see on certain television programs. Some of that
programming speaks to my heart and some of it does
not. There is a concept in America today that shocks
me. After everything we've endured, some people
judge other people because of their beliefs. By doing
so, they are behaving in a way that does not honor
basic Christian beliefs and boundaries. It is my hope
that I won't be judged because of my beliefs. It's so
easy to judge someone else for being different.
Embrace someone who is different. When you see
people who are angry, short-tempered, and hostile, it's
primarily because they are protecting themselves,
because their beliefs and boundaries are not strong
enough to protect their vulnerabilities. They lash out
in what they may perceive as self-defense before anyone has the chance to attack them. They feel weak-
ened by their lack of confidence. When you have the
absolute courage of your convictions, it becomes easier to face your life. When you are certain of your
beliefs and boundaries it is easier to live your life
knowing what you will do because there is much less
confusion. That comfort allows us to have relationships with and to be closer to people who think differently than we do. We can be open. We can hear.
We don't have to operate from a fearful place. When
people shut other people out, it's usually because of

fear. Great prejudice is born of fear. When I see someone who prejudges someone else, I see a person who
doesn't have strong convictions about their own
beliefs. Once you take away excuses, you understand
that there is no real reason to judge someone or
mistreat them.

During one of my business trips, I had the opportunity to spend time with people who had not experienced much diversity. The team I work with is very
diverse. We have people of all different backgrounds,
ethnicities, and beliefs at Kathy Ireland WorldWide.
We work together and we accomplish great things
in spite of how different we are. Each of us is able to
hold on to our individual beliefs and respect one
another because of them. We've been able to find a
commonality among ourselves that causes people to
come to us and ask what is it that we have that is so
special? They want to know how it works. What is it
about? That opens the door for me to talk about my
faith. Someone once asked me how I can work with
such a diverse group of people and still be Christian?
My answer is simple. *Because* I am Christian, it's very
easy to be involved with people who don't always
share my faith or think the same way I do.

I am the kind of person who is conscientious
about separating my business and personal life. For
me, the two often overlap in the sense that my

business partners are my family of choice. But when I am home with my husband and children, I like to place my focus on them. I've seen situations where everything can get triangulated—people get too close to the people they work with, and it comes back to haunt and hurt you in some way. For the longest time, I never called my partners unless it was business related. I always chose to keep a distance between business and personal issues. Even though that has changed over the years, we still respect the boundaries I have set about trying not to bring my work into the time I want to spend with my family. I feel that my family time has to be respected, especially while I have young children. Honoring your needs does not make you needy.

In life, hope for the best, plan for the worst. I believe that for me, business needs to serve the family rather than the family serve the business. Our boundaries will change and grow with us. When I became a mother, I found that there were certain business relationships that were not appropriate to my new role. As you know, there were people who said I was foolish to walk away from the money, but no amount of money can buy the peace that I have knowing that I am living according to my beliefs and boundaries. Discover, live, and practice your bound-aries and beliefs. There will always be obligations and pressures out there. I understand that. I have learned and also understand that beliefs and boundaries are powerful.

LESSON SEVEN

If we don't understand our value, our beliefs and boundaries will not protect us.

* Figure out your values ahead of time, so you won't ever find yourself in a compromising position and not know what to do.

* Setting boundaries will keep your priorities in order.

* Hope for the best, plan for the worst.

* Honoring your needs doesn't make you needy.

* Wise people constantly discover what they believe.

* Discover, live, and practice your boundaries and beliefs.

Chapter Eight

POWERFUL
JOYS AND SORROWS

❖ ❖

Life is filled with peaks and valleys. Without sorrow, true joy cannot be understood. I have experienced both. Every moment we live is a gift, and we must not take those moments for granted. Life can change in an instant, sometimes for the better and, sadly, sometimes for the worse. That is the balance of life. When people are constantly unhappy, I think they might be neglecting the gifts that God has given them. I believe that God gives everyone certain gifts. When you figure out what those are and how to use them, that's when you will have the most fulfilling and happiest life.

By now you know I really love kids. When I participate in something that involves children, I get really motivated and passionate about it. Working with talented teams as we design our children's home collection has given me a profound sense of joy. I call it the joy of accomplishment. Knowing that children may enjoy and sometimes benefit from our work is wonderful. It makes so many things possible. Recently my flooring partners at Shaw joined with me to develop a carpet collection called Kathy's Kids. All of the KIWW earnings from this collection will go to nonprofit organizations that serve children. That's a powerful joy.

Spending time with my husband and children is one of my greatest joys. On the day of the World Trade Center catastrophe, the experience of being clear across the country—far away from my husband and son, as well as the rest of my family—changed my perspective on everything. I was with my daughter, Lily, and my mother-in-law, Barbara Olsen. I was grateful to be with my daughter, but felt guilty that I had put her in this uncertain situation. My desire to be close to my family was never greater than it was on September 11, 2001. Though the town we were stranded in was peaceful, the situation in our country was not. It was comforting being with Lily and Barbara. My friends Miles and Rosemary and my in-laws, Grant, Dyan, and Wyatt, were so kind and supportive, but even with faith and friends beside us it was frightening not to know when we would be able to reconnect with my husband and son. My father was going through a particularly difficult time, facing a health crisis. My mother, who usually travels with me, stayed in California to be with Dad. I thought about renting a car to drive across the country since they weren't allowing airplanes to take off. While I was merely inconvenienced and scared, it is impossible to compare my fear and sorrow with those people who experienced true horror and tragedy. No matter how much we create a facade that we are different from other people, when it comes down to truly tragic situations, we are all in this life, this world, this experience together.

When we finally got the proper clearance to fly, we traveled through the night and were able to get back safely to Los Angeles a few days after the attacks. It was such a wonderful feeling and a true blessing to be reunited with my family. The moment I walked through the door, all I could do was look at my son sleeping and hold my husband. Finally, reunited and safe. I could feel the presence of true faith. The greatest gift God has given me is my family. Though I always had an appreciation for all of my personal blessings, after the attacks I was reminded of how precious each moment our time on earth is. In moments of joy, life's hassles seem to disappear. It is important to learn to make happy memories.

There was so much talk about getting back to normal after the attacks on America. I am not sure that we will ever be able to do that, and in a way,

I pray that we don't. It is my hope that people hold onto their new or restored faith. I love seeing the American flag flying. I enjoy the sense of patriotism. I have transcended what used to be normal and have found my way into desiring to make better decisions about where and with whom I spend my time. I recognize that I am fortunate to be able to have that kind of choice. In the aftermath of the attacks, the reality of how finite our time on earth is has crystallized in my mind. My focus has been sharpened. There is power in sorrow. That kind of sorrow is an opportunity to strengthen our faith. It can be changed into wisdom, which, if it does not bring joy, can certainly bring understanding which may lead to happiness at a later time.

It is our right as Americans to pursue happiness. This is something that should be appreciated. Once you have happiness, you no longer have the need to pursue it. It is yours to keep. There can be no true happiness or measure of a successful life that does not include service to others. The importance of that service has nothing to do with public recognition. Our lives are filled with joy when we live in the truth that we've made a positive difference in the world around us. That kind of joy is something everyone can experience.

The significance of September 11 has been a common thread throughout this book. As I have said in previous chapters, the impact of that day has been ever present in everything since, but it really didn't change the way I lived. It affected how I think. It shifted my appreciation of being an American. I realized that my faith helped me not to feel rage, but rather pain. There have been flashes of anger, but mostly I feel pain for the loss of life and of the sense of freedom and stability many of us took for granted before that day. I feel hurt for the tremendous devastation. It was a reminder to me that there is evil in the world, which is a very hard thing to have to see and comprehend.

It's important to know that God does not cause these evil things to happen. We were all born with the gift of free will. From the beginning of time, people have made bad choices. We cannot blame the world's atrocities on God. We ask, how can God be loving and just and allow these things to happen? I believe these things happen as a result of people turning away from God. I don't have the answers for why in some situations God intervenes and why in others He does not. There are things about this world that I don't understand and I realize that many of my questions will not be answered until I get to Heaven.

. . . HE LEARNED OBEDIENCE FROM
WHAT HE SUFFERED . . . .
Hebrews 5:8

It's a tremendous feeling standing tall on one of life's peaks while enjoying the view. It's equally lonely finding yourself at the bottom of one of life's valleys. I cannot eradicate the image of the World Trade Center standing tall one moment and crumbling to the ground the next. The symbolism of the twin towers being reduced to a mountain of debris and becoming what we now refer to as Ground Zero is one of the most profound images of the fragility of life in recent history.

Sadly for many of us, it takes a catastrophic event to understand the power of faith and the power of God. As painful as it may be, sorrow is the great equalizer of life. It certainly is used as such throughout the Bible. The story of Job, a righteous man who suffered more than anyone could ever imagine, is the best example I can think of to illustrate that there isn't always an answer we understand to why tragic events occur. Regardless of how challenging it got for Job, he clung to God and God rewarded him. He never wavered in his faith. A tragic event often brings us closer to God and strengthens our faith. Does God want us to shift our focus from what we want from Him to humbly depending on Him in good times as well as tragic moments? That question certainly has the power to fortify. I have met so many people in my life who have suffered terrible pain, loss, and tragedy. Yet these are some of the strongest people I know. I would expect to find anger and bitterness because of their circumstances. Instead, I find a solace and strength in the way they live. Sorrow is a bit like a gift that nobody wants. For some, it takes being brought to our knees to see the truth.

One of my private sorrows came prior to the birth of my daughter, Lily. My husband and I had been trying to have another baby. While at a photo shoot, I became ill and was rushed to an emergency room, only to discover that I had been pregnant, but had miscarried. The sorrow of losing this child was devastating. I never had the chance to celebrate the pregnancy. I had lost a child and mourned. I had never known a greater sorrow. It was the death of a loved one. To our delight, however, I conceived a short time thereafter, and we were told that the baby had tested positive for Down's syndrome. Our doctor reassured us that a lot of times that test could show a false positive. We were simply thrilled about the pregnancy and we would love our baby no matter what challenges he or she was born with. We knew that God would bless us with the beautiful child we were meant to have with or without Down's. Either way, we would love and care for this child. I believe that all babies are perfect. God doesn't make mistakes. When our doctor suggested that I have amniocentesis to see if the baby indeed had Down's syndrome, I felt it was wrong. It was inconceivable for me to decide the fate of my unborn child based on any test. Whatever the results, there was nothing that would be able to help the baby in our situation. It would only satisfy the curiosity of whether or not our baby was going to be born with challenges. Even with the seed of doubt from the Down's syndrome test, I refused to have the amniocentesis. There is a very small risk of a miscarriage due to the amniocentesis test. Even though the percentage of miscarriages is tiny, it was not worth the risk to me.

During my pregnancy, I continued to work with the Special Olympics and Eunice Kennedy Shriver, who has always inspired me through her tireless efforts to teach the world to embrace human beings with special needs. They're wonderfully unique people—just like every one of God's children. Knowing about the Special Olympics and being involved with them gave me a great deal of comfort during my pregnancy.

For four years, I was also involved with the March of Dimes, serving as the honorary chair for their

"Walk America" campaign. Every participant in the walkathon is a real hero, turning their hearts toward helping the most vulnerable and innocent of all beings. It's heartbreaking to see families watch their baby struggle so fiercely to survive. While working with the March of Dimes, I visited several families who are so inspiring. Experiencing this has galvanized our resolve to join the fight for these young lives. During my pregnancy, I knew in my heart, as I spent time with these families, that I might easily become a parent faced with raising a child born with a birth defect. It was both a joyous and scary time in our lives. In spite of our doctor's concerns, our daughter Lily was born a happy, healthy baby.

As the honorary chair of the March of Dimes Walk America program, I had the opportunity to visit neonatal intensive care units across the country. I had the opportunity to actually hold babies in my hand who were born as early as twenty-six weeks. These little fighters literally fit in the palm of my hand. These were babies who under normal circumstances would reside in their mother's womb another three months. Surfactant therapy, developed by March of Dimes research, helps these babies to survive. This, along with fetal surgery, which is also due to March of Dimes research, clearly demonstrates to me the humanity of the unborn.

Last year, I ended my relationship with the March of Dimes when we couldn't agree on their position regarding human fetal tissue research. The fact that the March of Dimes conducted research on human fetal tissue from aborted babies was something that I had not been aware of. It is my belief that all babies are of value and worth fighting for whether they are wanted or not. I am so aware of the wonderful research opportunities that exist in the world of science. I understand the need for fetal tissue research as an exploratory option. My objection is only to research studies that involve elective abortion. Still-births and spontaneous abortions are all tragedies that may offer scientific opportunities while not condoning the taking of a life. There are many exciting breakthroughs in the medical community involving adult stem cells, blood from the umbilical cord, and human fat cells—none of these procedures puts a human life at risk. We must continue to find cures to all diseases. I believe we will find cures in ethical research.

After months of dialogue with the March of Dimes people, I made my decision. And it brought me both peace and sorrow. Before making my decision I began gathering facts about this research. While gathering my facts, a friend asked me, if someone I loved were in peril, would I use a drug or procedure that had been created from the research that I chose to distance myself from? Tough question. Fair question. I believe I would not. I pray I would not. I never want to be hypocritical.

There have been so many times in my life when I have not always understood God's reasons for certain things that happen. I asked the parents of a young boy I knew who had recently passed away if they thought their son had been angry with God before he died. They said that he hadn't been angry so much as he was confused. He had so many questions before he passed on and wasn't able to get all of his answers. As I've come to know God better, I now understand that He's not tormenting me in any way by making life sometimes harder than I would like it to be. Celebrate the joy in life as strongly as you mourn the sorrows. When I miscarried, I found comfort, as hard as it was, in the fact that it was part of God's bigger plan, and, for some reason, He needed this little person up there with Him. I didn't even know I was pregnant when we lost the baby, but we were heartbroken. Though I don't know why, I am certain that someday when I get up there, I will find His reason. I must trust that we're not meant to understand everything that happens to us, but God knows exactly what He is doing.

For me, this year has been a really challenging year, personally and in business. It's important to let yourself feel losses, and move forward. If you have a business setback, you need to come to terms with it quickly so you don't take that loss into the next meeting. Otherwise, you may have another loss right off the bat. It's also important to celebrate the joys with team members, with everyone involved in the success of a project. I have learned to endure the roller-coaster ride of success and failure much like I deal with joy and sorrow. As an entrepreneur, I have learned to take it all in stride. Business, like life, is cyclical. As long as I feel like I am doing a service for others, that I give of myself in ways I wouldn't otherwise be able to do, I will continue on my journey as an entrepreneur. There will be hurtful disappointments and that is part of the process.

After a project I recently did, I eagerly awaited the feedback. I was hopeful that the people would be kind and they weren't. It was a personal setback for me. I couldn't help but talk about it with some of the other people involved. Someone suggested a piece of advice I will never forget. He told me that I needed to place a tiny callus over my heart every time I read or heard a cruel remark about myself, because eventually that callus would be hard and strong and my heart wouldn't feel the pain. I thought about his words for a few moments, and I realized that I didn't want to have a callused heart. If I couldn't feel the pain, I would never be able to understand the pleasure of positive feedback. It became clear to me that there is a natural ebb and flow in the world. We have to celebrate the joy in our lives just as we must mourn the sorrow. Learning to keep it all in perspective and not letting that pendulum swing too far on either side is the key to keeping balance in my life.

If I suffer a loss in business, I can't simply stop living or functioning. If I did, I'd be out of business in no time. I deal with challenges in business by trying to keep my mind-set and level of enthusiasm at the same place as when I began selling rocks from my little red wagon. It all boils down to our point of view. How we see things is as important as what it is we are looking at. Allowing ourselves to be open to sorrow as well as joy is reminiscent of our humanity. It is so easy to get lost in our drive for success, a drive that can become very insular and isolating. We must never lose sight of our priorities.

I once heard a quote by Betty Bender who said, "when people go to work, they shouldn't have to leave their hearts at home." I couldn't agree with her more on that issue. I personally believe that being an entrepreneur is about being of service, and I never want to leave my heart at home. I want to take my heart with me every day. I have tried to instill that way of thinking into my everyday living as a wife, mother, and businesswoman. Success in business and in life depends on people. As people we must depend on each other. I want to foster an environment at work and at home where the people I surround myself with are people who have heart. Knowing who you can turn to in times of trouble is essential in getting through those periods. Number one on my list is God. Sometimes we can allow our fear or sorrow to escalate to the point of defeat. When my children have those nights where they can't sleep because they are afraid, I remind them of the serenity prayer: "God grant me the serenity to accept the things I cannot change. Courage to change the things I can and wisdom to know the difference." When we've assessed the situation and made sure we've done everything possible to address the scariness, then I give my children a piece of advice I hope they will always carry with them: "Keep your eyes upon Jesus." I love the story in Matthew 14:22–32 about Jesus walking on water out to His disciples who were in a boat on a lake. Peter got so excited he wanted to do it too. As long as he kept his eyes on Jesus, he was able to walk on water. But the moment he took his eyes off the Lord and started focusing on his circumstances, he became afraid and began to sink. We can sink in the hopelessness of our situation, or keep our eyes on Jesus who can pull us out of any storm.

Real joy is not based on circumstances or a situation. Real joy is something that cannot be taken away. Even in the midst of our grieving, deep in our heart, we can have the joy of knowing whatever painful situation we are in we may be fearful but we are not alone. The Lord is always with us. Romans 5:3–5 tells us ". . . but we also rejoice in our sufferings, because we know that suffering produces perseverance; perseverance, character; and character, hope. And hope does not disappoint us, because God has poured out His love into our hearts by the Holy Spirit, whom He has given us." As with the sorrow I have felt in my life, I have had great joy. Sometimes that joy emerged like the sun shining through the clouds. I have been given so much. I am blessed to share the joy of knowing my two wonderful parents well into my adult life. If I turn out to be one tiny fraction of the mom that my mom is, that would be an amazing accomplishment for me. I depend on my mom in so many ways. She does everything with such ease. Mom cleaned the house while whistling and singing. She never made us feel guilty for taking care of us. I will always appreciate that. As a child I took Mom for granted because I thought all moms were like that. It wasn't until I started playing at my friends' homes that I realized how incredibly special my mom was. In a way, I felt bad for everyone else because they couldn't have my mom for a mom. I see my mom as a missionary. She travels with me all the time. Everywhere we go, people adopt her. If they sit next to her on a plane, they just open right up to her. She's not judgmental so I think people feel safe telling her things. She's a very gentle and loving woman. She comes from such an honest and understanding place. She has amazing insight and wisdom, which comes from years of nurturing others. As I get older, I find that encouraging.

I don't look forward to my body falling apart with age or not being able to do things that I might take for granted today, but I do look forward to growing and blossoming with age like my mother. I think that's what keeps her so young, vivacious, and beautiful. She's constantly learning and is so full of adventure. Mom told me that as she got older, she started praying for more energy. She's gotten much younger since becoming a grandmother. She jumps on the bed with the kids and makes forts out of blankets and pillows.

After I had Lily, Mom started talking about the biblical story of Sarah. In the story, Sarah wanted desperately to have children, but was not able to become pregnant. After a lifetime of believing she would never become pregnant, Sarah discovered in her eighties that she was going to be a mother. Mom and I were talking about what her fears must have been facing motherhood at such a late stage in her life. As it is, I get tired at the end of a fun-filled day with my kids. I can't even imagine becoming a mother for the first time in my eighties! Mom explained to me that her energy was a necessity if she was going to become involved with my kids in the way that she is. It's fun to see and the kids love that she can keep up with them. She sings the same songs to them that she used to sing to my sisters and me when we were children. It is a wonderfully powerful joy to witness her bliss.

Erik, Lily, and Chloe are my three greatest joys. For a brief time after Lily was born, Erik didn't share the same excitement as the rest of the family for our new arrival. I would come downstairs in the morning, and he'd tell me to go away! My husband would try to explain to Erik that he had to be respectful, but I understood that he felt threatened by his baby sister. I felt such joy holding my daughter, and at the same time I felt terribly guilty for my son's anger toward me. Of course, my hormones were in a postpartum rage and my emotions were out of control anyway, but I couldn't help feeling like I had gained a daughter, whom I love so much, fearing I might be losing my son's love. About ten days after Lily was born, while I was driving Erik to school, he informed me that after school was over that day he planned on running away from home. I had read every parenting book that suggests you tell your child that you'd be happy to help him pack, but all I could do was pull the car over and start to sob. I begged Erik not to run away and told him that I would be so sad if he left. I did everything I knew I wasn't supposed to do. He looked at me as if I was really losing my mind! I think I kind of freaked him out, but I couldn't help it. A few days later, it was as if some burden had been lifted off his little shoulders, and my son realized that his sister was a part of our family and she was going to be a person who would live with us forever, and who we would all love forever. Lily, in spite of his great fear, was not there to wreck his life. I am happier spending time with my family than I am in any other situation. I love to spend individual time with my husband and kids. Too often we expect joy to be spontaneous. Just as I believe love is a verb I believe that powerful joy is something that we sometimes need to plan for and work toward. One-on-one time is so important and I like to plan dates—days where I spend that perfect time alone with my husband, my son, or my daughter. We pick a day, and I let the kids choose whatever it is that will bring them joy. Having our children actively participate in our family plans empowers them and makes us a happier family. There is no competition between the kids for my attention, because they know that on that special day I am there for them, and only them. I get to know them better when we share that one-on-one time. Dates with our children don't have to cost money or be elaborate to be fun. Lily likes to swim with me, play at the beach, and read books and play make-believe. My good friend Sue is teaching Lily how to swim, and she likes to pretend she's a mermaid or a princess and I usually have to be the villain. They both love finding frogs and lizards. When Erik was five years old we had a date where he chose to play in our yard. We had had a lot of rain so that meant we would play in the mud. As I looked at Erik rolling in the mud, covered from head to toe like a little piggy, he looked up at me and said, "Mom, this is the best day of my life." A priceless memory and a powerful joy.

That's the way my parents were with my sisters and me growing up. That's how I learned the pleasure of simple joy. I don't believe kids need a lot of toys or video games to keep them happy. We go camping and hiking together. That's one of our favorite family activities. We all love it. The kids collect leaves and rocks and they get to use their imaginations.

Seeing joy through my children's eyes is a daily reminder of the importance of celebrating life and all its blessings. We are all capable of living lives characterized by great joy. Within each of us is an amazing human spirit that is strong enough to overcome pain, disappointment, and sorrow. No matter what our current situation happens to be, or what beliefs we may currently harbor about ourselves, we can tap into that inner strength and wisdom and move forward to allow God to create more joy in our daily living. At times, we may diminish our ability to experience joy by being preoccupied with the past or even momentary sorrow. Regardless of the situation, someone, somewhere, has already faced a similar set of circumstances and has found a way to bring joy back into his or her life. There is always a light at the end of the tunnel shining from Heaven.

Most of the successful people I know have suffered disappointments or setbacks, if not total and utter failure—myself included. Everyone experiences loss. It comes with the joy of being human. What also comes with the package is our ability to prevail over any challenge and use our personal experiences for growth. There comes a point in each of our lives when we must realize that we are responsible for our own joy. Long-lasting happiness doesn't come from another person, your job, where you live, or how much money you make. We can make a conscious decision to have joy in our lives regardless of our situations. Living in day-to-day joy comes from understanding our basic human needs and developing ways to meet them. For me, it is the understanding that I am never alone. God is there to lift me up when I fall.

My joy is rooted in knowing I will spend eternity with Christ. No matter how horrible my day might be, no one can take that joy away.

There are many factors in life that we cannot control. Your amazing spirit is strong enough to overcome any obstacle. The world is forever changing. Relationships cycle through phases of push and pull, schedules become hectic, plans are made and then thwarted, weather doesn't cooperate, the house needs work, your job seems impossible to do, and the list goes on and on. It becomes a waste of time to hold ourselves and others to a standard of perfection that is based on an image or thought of the way things are supposed to be. There is no second guessing God and *His* plan. Allowing ourselves to be open to sorrow will also keep us open to our greatest potential for joy. Please learn to play more. Learn to relax. Ease up a little. Try new things. Don't be afraid of failing. Connect with the beauty of the world. Make each day special. Help someone in need. Most of all, make time to be appreciative of God and *His* great glory. I guarantee that your life will change. Your burdens of sorrow will be lifted from your shoulders and you will live a more joyful life filled with love and blessings.

LESSON EIGHT

We are all capable of living our lives with great joy.

- Sorrow is a great equalizer in life.
- Celebrate the joy in life as strongly as you mourn the sorrows.
- The strongest people I know have triumphed over tragedies.
- Without sorrow, true joy cannot be understood.
- Your amazing spirit is strong enough to overcome any obstacle.
- There is no second guessing God and His plan.
- Learn to play.
- Learn to relax.
- Learn new things.
- Learn to let go.
- Help someone in need.

Powerful Inspirations

LESSON RECAP

◈ ◈

Inspiration
ALL THINGS ARE POSSIBLE
WITH GOD.
(Mark 10:27)

LESSON ONE

Faith is the key to stability and the cornerstone of life.

- Life is tough. Faith will get you through the tough times.
- When God is with us, who can be against us?
- Never compromise your character to achieve any goal.
- Faith takes courage and is rewarded.
- Character is a path, not a destination.
- Faith is everlasting.
- The Bible is the greatest book ever written for managing life.

Inspiration

LET US RUN WITH PERSEVERANCE
THE RACE MARKED OUT FOR US.

Hebrews 12:1

LESSON TWO

*Success in life is achieved by experiencing and
conquering challenges.*

- The power of you . . . you are powerful.

- If self-esteem comes from superficial things, we will
  be disappointed.

- True self-esteem is attainable by everyone.

- Failure is an education.

- Find and live your passion.

- Celebrate our differences.

- Don't think less of yourself, think of yourself less.

- Even with great self-esteem you will get hurt from
  time to time.

Inspiration

TRAIN A CHILD IN THE WAY HE
SHOULD GO, AND WHEN HE IS OLD
HE WILL NOT TURN FROM IT.

Proverbs 22:6

LESSON THREE

A strong family foundation will influence you and your loved ones for life.

- Things you learn as a child and teach as a parent last a lifetime.

- It takes years to build trust and respect, but a moment to destroy it.

- We learn our deepest truths through our relationships.

- There are two kinds of families—the family we are born into and the family we choose.

- With family you are never alone.

Inspiration

ASK AND IT WILL BE GIVEN TO YOU;
SEEK AND YOU WILL FIND.

Matthew 7:7–8

LESSON FOUR

Powerful answers come from meaningful and important questions.

- When someone tells you no, ask why. When someone tells you yes, ask how.

- Overcome your fears to ask questions and seek information.

- You must ask for what you need.

- Be a good listener.

- Be quick to listen; slow to speak; and slow to become angry.

- Some of the best questions I hear come from children—their innocence illuminates.

- When you ask powerful questions, you get powerful answers. We need to be ready for them.

◈ ◈

Inspiration

FOR I HAVE LEARNED TO BE CONTENT
WHATEVER THE CIRCUMSTANCES
Phil 4:11

LESSON FIVE

Change is the only certainty in life.

- Change forces us out of our comfort zone.

- Celebrate positive changes. Work through negative ones to discover something positive in them.

- When God is on the back burner, everything falls out of balance.

- Why not you?

- Don't let fear hold you back.

- Keep your eye on the big picture.

- It's great to have goals, but don't forget to enjoy the journey.

- Growth means preparing for change.

- Prepare for change. It will happen.

- History doesn't change. Perspectives do.

Inspiration

BLESSED IS THE MAN WHO FINDS
WISDOM, THE MAN WHO GAINS
UNDERSTANDING, FOR HE IS MORE
PROFITABLE THAN SILVER AND YIELDS
BETTER RETURNS THAN GOLD.

Proverbs 3:13

LESSON SIX

*Live beneath your means, and you will always have
enough money.*

* Each one of us has, is, or will experience financial
  difficulties in our lives.

* Financial independence is important.

* Money can create comfort and opportunity—
  nothing more.

* Money won't solve all your problems.

* Own money; never let it own you.

* Having money is not a sin; loving money is.

◈ ◈

Inspiration

WHEN A FLOOD CAME,
THE TORRENT STRUCK THAT HOUSE
BUT COULD NOT SHAKE IT,
BECAUSE IT WAS WELL BUILT.

Luke 6:4–8

LESSON SEVEN

If we don't understand our value, our beliefs and boundaries will not protect us.

- Figure out your values ahead of time, so you won't ever find yourself in a compromising position and not know what to do.

- Setting boundaries will keep your priorities in order.

- Hope for the best, plan for the worst.

- Honoring your needs doesn't make you needy.

- Wise people constantly discover what they believe.

- Discover, live, and practice your boundaries and beliefs.

Inspiration

CONSIDER IT PURE JOY, MY BROTHERS,
WHENEVER YOU FACE TRIALS OF ANY KIND.

James 1:2

LESSON EIGHT

We are all capable of living our lives with great joy.

* Sorrow is a great equalizer in life.

* Celebrate the joy in life as strongly as you mourn
  the sorrows.

* The strongest people I know have triumphed
  over tragedies.

* Without sorrow, true joy cannot be understood.

* Your amazing spirit is strong enough to overcome
  any obstacle.

* There is no second guessing God and His plan.

* Learn to play.

* Learn to relax.

* Learn new things.

* Learn to let go.

* Help someone in need.

KATHY IRELAND is one of America's most accomplished entrepreneurial CEOs. She is the recipient of the Businesswoman of the Year Award from the National Association of Women Business Owners, and she received an Outstanding Mother of the Year Award from the National Mother's Day Committee. Her brand has garnered the legendary Good Housekeeping Seal for consumer excellence. She lives in California with her husband, Greg, and their three children, Erik, Lily, and Chloe.

LAURA MORTON is the author of seventeen books and has written six *New York Times* bestsellers. She lives in New York.